THE
CLASSIC
MEDITERRANEAN
COOKBOOK

SARAH WOODWARD

THE
CLASSIC
MEDITERRANEAN
COOKBOOK

DORLING KINDERSLEY
London • New York • Stuttgart

A DORLING KINDERSLEY BOOK

Editor
Lorna Damms

Art Editor
Jo Grey

Designer
Helen Diplock

DTP Designer
Karen Ruane

Managing Editor
Susannah Marriott

Senior Managing Art Editor
Carole Ash

Photography
Clive Streeter
Dave King

Home Economist
Janice Murfitt

Production Controller
Lauren Britton

First published in Great Britain in 1995
by Dorling Kindersley Limited
9 Henrietta Street, London WC2E 8PS

Copyright © 1995
Dorling Kindersley Limited, London
Text copyright © 1995 Sarah Woodward

All rights reserved. No part of this publication may be
reproduced, stored in a retrieval system, or transmitted in
any form or by any means, electronic, mechanical,
photocopying, recording or otherwise, without the prior
written permission of the copyright owner.

A CIP catalogue record for this book is available
from the British Library
ISBN 0 7513 0214 7

Reproduced in Singapore by Colourscan
Printed and bound in Italy by A. Mondadori, Verona

CONTENTS

MARKET PRODUCE 10

*A vibrant full-colour guide to the key
ingredients used in Mediterranean cooking, with
advice on choosing, preparing and storing*

CLASSIC DISHES 32

*Authentic specialities from the eastern
and western Mediterranean, illustrated with
photographs of the finished dishes and
their ingredients*

INTRODUCTION

The countries of the Mediterranean enjoy a cuisine rooted deep in classical traditions. This, after all, was the sea criss-crossed by the Minoans, Phoenicians, Ancient Greeks and Romans, as each built their empires. Then came the Arabs, with their love of market gardens and fruits. For centuries the countries bordering this bountiful sea may have suffered under conquering armies, but they also found themselves on major trade routes.

The cooks travelling with these armies and courts brought new ideas for the kitchen. The fish soups that are now found throughout the region are credited to the Greeks, while Arabs taught the Sicilians to make water-ices. There is even a hotly disputed theory that the Romans were introduced to the art of pasta-making by the Chinese. With the precious cargoes from the East and India arrived exciting new foodstuffs, supplementing the basic crops of wheat, olives and grapes; not just spices, but citrus fruit, melons, aubergines, peaches and pomegranates. And if the discovery of the "New World" at the end of the 15th century led to a collapse in the old trading empires, it did not halt the flow of new ingredients carried back by the different armies – tomatoes, peppers and beans being some of the most important introductions.

The Mediterranean region has always enjoyed a cross-fertilization of culinary ideas and the gastronomic borders are still blurred. In Sicily you can eat a fish couscous that bears a remarkable similarity to that served over the water in Tunisia; you can enjoy figs baked in honey in Provence just as well as in Greece. And if there are similarities, there are also constants – wherever you are in the Mediterranean, you will find olives, bread, lemons, herbs and spices. For whichever port those seafaring cooks landed at, they found similar growing conditions. Long hot summers and dry winters mean that, despite its apparent lushness in spring, this has always been a harsh region for farmers. As a result, the Mediterranean diet, lacking rich butter, cream and meat-based dishes, is often described as austere, even sober. To me it is anything but that. Looking at the riot of colour on the market stalls, the bunches of glossy green herbs, the vibrant shades of the fruit, I am instead struck by the abundance of the region. Even in the middle of an arid summer, away from the crowded tourist beaches the air is heavy with the scent of the herbs growing wild on the hillsides.

The life of the Mediterranean lies in the mountains that rear above the pine groves, in the small hill-top villages and particularly in the busy cities that ring its shore. It is here that you will still find the

kind of meal most of us dream of when we think of the
Mediterranean. You may be sitting on a terrace overlooking the
sea, in a little market café, or in the dark cool kitchen of a friend.
The meal will start with something to nibble at with a glass of wine,
perhaps a few olives and some spicy dips served with warm bread.
There may be a pasta dish laden with garlic and herbs, some grilled
fish or meat cooked over charcoal and, to refresh your palate, a
bowl of fresh fruit on ice. If the weather is cooler, you may start
with a thick soup scattered with Parmesan, followed by a casserole
laden with spices, and, to finish, a sticky pastry served with a cup of
steaming coffee.

There is no need to restrict this kind of meal to an idyllic memory.
It is easy to create a Mediterranean meal at home, provided you
obey one basic rule: take care to buy the best quality seasonal
ingredients. The Mediterranean peoples are great shoppers. This
attribute above all others characterizes the quality of their food.

I have brought together here recipes from throughout the region,
from its very western shores to its eastern limits. They are all my
favourites. For this is food that is good for you, easy to prepare
and a delight to look at as well as to eat – reflecting the great
classical traditions of the Mediterranean.

A HEALTHY WAY OF EATING

The main crops of the Mediterranean have always been wheat, olives and vines, and from these core products come the principles of Mediterranean eating. The classic snack is still a hunk of coarse bread (perhaps rubbed with tomato or garlic), dunked in olive oil, accompanied by a glass of red wine and followed by fresh fruit.

Nutritionists, after decades of study, have come to believe that this simple diet is positively beneficial. Its merits stem from the heavy emphasis on cereals, fresh fruit, vegetables and fish, and from the limited amounts of dairy products and meat eaten. Evidence even appears to indicate that red wine, consumed in moderation, may have a positive effect in the avoidance of heart disease.

OLIVE OIL

The Mediterranean diet results in part from the climate and terrain. This area is not conducive to cattle rearing, so olive oil takes the place of butter. High in mono-unsaturated fats and easy to digest, olive oil is believed to be one of the best cooking mediums. Of course, it should be consumed in moderation, for it has just as high a calorie and kilojoule count as other fats and oils.

FRUIT AND VEGETABLES

Fresh vegetables and fruit are important sources of vitamins, and studies have shown that they may even offer protection against certain chronic diseases. In the Mediterranean, most fruit is eaten raw, as part of the daily diet, and vegetables are used in abundance. The typically simple preparation is also beneficial; some vitamins leach out during cooking, but if fresh produce is cooked briefly and served with its cooking liquids, few nutrients are lost. The ubiquitous garlic is an important ingredient as it contains allicin – a substance that appears to lower blood pressure and cholesterol.

PULSES, CEREALS AND PASTA

Pulses are an excellent source of protein, contain iron and are high in soluble fibre and low in fat. When pulses are eaten with cereals, the combination provides a "complete" protein, as nutritionally valuable as fish or meat, as in Tuscan bean and pasta soup or the rice and lentil dishes of the eastern Mediterranean. Cereals provide the bulk in the Mediterranean diet. The flour that is milled from the locally produced wheat is not too highly refined, giving a unique flavour and consistency to the typical country-style breads that accompany most meals.

The durum wheat used in pasta is full of proteins and vitamins and so a dish of pasta with a vegetable sauce is both healthy and, because it is high in carbohydrates, sustaining. Durum wheat is also consumed as couscous in North Africa, while bulgur wheat is common to the east of the region. Rice, another staple, is a valuable source of carbohydrates, protein and B vitamins.

MEAT AND DAIRY PRODUCE

Sheep and goats are the region's main livestock and are as important for their milk as for their flesh. Milk is rarely consumed fresh, but is used to make yogurts and cheeses. Pigs are also farmed and pork is often cured to make salamis and hams, which are eaten in small quantities. Little is wasted; nutrient-high offal is widely available. Poultry, a low-fat meat, is very popular and lean game is a valued resource. But, like dairy products, meat is as likely to be used as a flavouring as to constitute the main element of a meal.

FISH AND SHELLFISH

Fish is often the central element of a meal and is an important protein source. It is especially useful in "completing" the vegetable proteins provided by cereals – a little fish served with pasta or bread allows the digestive system to benefit in full from the protein offering. Popular oily fish like the sardine and mackerel are rich in essential fatty acids which help protect against heart disease and promote health generally. The usual way to prepare fish is to grill or bake it, which is also the healthiest approach.

Perhaps, above all, it is the Mediterranean peoples' overall attitude to food that makes their way of eating so healthy. Food is taken seriously here. Time is spent both in its preparation and consumption, producing well-balanced meals to share with family and friends.

Market Produce

One of the great pleasures of being in the
Mediterranean is shopping in the markets that dot its
shores. The cooking of the region is founded on the
seasonal local produce, be it fish fresh from the sea
or sun-ripened fruit and vegetables. Many dishes
are prepared very simply to allow the flavours to shine
through, so the quality of the ingredients is a prime
consideration. The Mediterranean cook is above
all a discerning shopper.

VEGETABLES

The Mediterranean market is a colourful sight all year round because throughout the region, vegetables constitute a large part of the daily diet. Many vegetables owe their peculiar sweetness to having been sun-ripened and picked in their prime, and produce is used when in season and, therefore, when at its most flavourful.

OTHER TYPICAL VEGETABLES
beetroot, chicory, peas, potatoes (larger floury varieties and small waxy potatoes), Swiss chard, vine leaves, cardoons, horta (wild greens)

CUCUMBERS
Small ridged cucumbers have a firmer texture and are the most flavoursome. Tiny cucumbers pickle well.

Courgette flower

Flat bean

Marmande tomatoes

Plum tomatoes

Small cucumber

COURGETTES
Small courgettes are sweetest; larger fleshy ones can be bitter and should be salted before use. The orange flowers are delicious fried in olive oil.

TOMATOES
The tomato is central to Mediterranean cuisine. Plum tomatoes should be used for cooking and firm-fleshed Marmande or beef tomatoes in salads — the riper the better. Hot-house tomatoes cannot compete with those ripened in the sun.

Runner bean

BEANS
Broad beans, unless very young, have tough outer skins that should be removed. Long flat beans or runner beans are essential to paella. Choose crisp specimens and remove the fibrous strings before cooking. Haricot and borlotti beans are also enjoyed fresh, especially in France and Italy.

Broad beans

Radicchio

Cos

SALAD LEAVES
Mediterranean salads contain an infinite variety of small bitter leaves and sweet herbs, reflecting the variety growing in the wild. Rocket, dandelion leaves, chicory, purslane and lamb's lettuce frequently appear in salads, while cos, radicchio and frisée are popular larger lettuces.

VEGETABLES

AUBERGINES
It is difficult to imagine Mediterranean cooking without the aubergine, but when it was first brought from the East it took many years to become accepted. Choose plump but not over-long aubergines, with taut, glossy skins, and look out for unusual varieties, such as round white aubergines or the tiny pickling variety.

FENNEL
The dried branches of the wild fennel that grows in the hills surrounding the sea are often used to scent barbecues with their aniseed aroma. When using the cultivated Florence fennel, keep the feathery fronds for use as a herb.

Florence fennel

Green pepper

CELERY
Celery is usually eaten cooked. Look for celery with leaves attached — they are much used in Italian cooking.

Thin green sprues

White asparagus

PEPPERS
Introduced from the "New World", capsicum peppers, like the tomato, are today an integral part of Mediterranean food. They range in colour and shape from tapering pale green varieties through to bell-shaped dark green and sweeter red peppers.

Red pepper

ASPARAGUS
First cultivated by the Romans, asparagus grows wild in the Mediterranean region. The spindly green stalks (sprue) of the wild variety are prized by the Spanish, while the Italians prefer luscious fat white asparagus.

Rocket

Frisée

GLOBE ARTICHOKES
The globe artichoke, like its relative the cardoon, is a member of the thistle family. Tiny new season's artichokes are tender enough to be eaten whole. The hearts of the larger varieties are a seasonal delicacy.

Lamb's lettuce

13

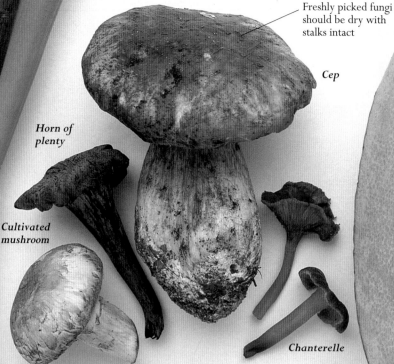

Freshly picked fungi should be dry with stalks intact

Cep

Horn of plenty

Cultivated mushroom

Chanterelle

MUSHROOMS

Gathering wild fungi is akin to a national sport in the western Mediterranean. The cep (porcini), the horn of plenty (trompette de mort) and the chanterelle are highly prized. Cultivated button and field mushrooms are also widely used.

Spring onion

BROCCOLI

This vegetable can be purple or white as well as green, which is the variety known in Italy as calabrese. The heads should be small and compact. It responds well to quick cooking.

LEEKS

Like their relative the onion, leeks play an important role as a basic flavouring in many dishes, such as vegetable soups, as well as being eaten as a vegetable in their own right. Always wash and trim leeks before use to remove any traces of grit.

Leek

Spanish onion

ONIONS

Large golden-skinned Spanish onions, white mild onions, sweet red onions, long spring onions and tiny pickling onions are much used in Mediterranean cooking. Keep them in a dark place and discard any that have started to sprout.

Red onion

PUMPKINS

Small pumpkins have sweeter flesh than overgrown ones, which can be fibrous. They are popular in savoury dishes as the flavour marries well with rich ingredients, herbs and spices.

The tender stalks of baby leaves do not need to be removed

SPINACH

Spinach leaves should be crisp and bright green, with no hint of yellow or sliminess. Cooking, which should be brief, vastly diminishes the bulk of this vitamin-rich vegetable. Baby leaves are good raw in salads.

CARROTS

Large, older carrots are generally preferred for their stronger flavour, especially in the eastern Mediterranean – the exception is if a dish calls for spring vegetables. Carrots should always be crisp and juicy when broken in half; discard any that feel soft or are wrinkled.

CABBAGES

First harvested by the Romans from a sea plant, cabbages are a staple vegetable in the Mediterranean. Look out for the cavolo nero or black cabbage, much used in Tuscan soups for its distinctive flavour, and the dark green savoy. Red cabbage is a popular winter salad leaf in Turkey.

Romanesco cauliflower

CAULIFLOWERS

Members of the cabbage family, cauliflowers can be found in various colours; vivid green pyramidal florets can be found as well as more typical white formations. Cauliflowers should be firm and even in colour – avoid any that are blemished or slightly soft.

Common cauliflower

TURNIPS

New season's turnips are small, sweet and tinged with pink. They can be eaten raw in salads or braised and then caramelized, and are often found in Moroccan couscous dishes. The Lebanese make a piquant turnip pickle.

Savoy cabbage

FRUIT AND NUTS

Fresh and dried fruit is an essential component of the Mediterranean diet. A selection of chilled fresh fruit is the most typical and delicious way to end a meal, and out of season a bowl of dried fruit and nuts may be offered. Both fruit and nuts are used in savoury and sweet dishes, especially in North Africa and the east of the region.

OTHER TYPICAL FRUIT
apricots; cherries; pears, such as comice and conference; tangerines, satsumas and clementines; persimmons, or sharon fruit; bilberries; currants

Wild strawberries

STRAWBERRIES
Huge crops of early strawberries are grown in Spain in particular. In Italy and southern France, look out for the more aromatic little wild strawberries from the woods.

POMEGRANATES
The pomegranate's sour, perfumed juice is used in savoury dishes in the eastern Mediterranean.

Mirabelles

Purple plum

PLUMS
Eaten both fresh and cooked, plums originate from Europe and are found in many varieties, from tiny sweet yellow mirabelles to large juicy purple plums. In their dried form as prunes, they are used to enrich savoury dishes.

PEACHES
If a peach is ripe, its skin will peel away easily; avoid any that are bruised. White peaches and white smooth-skinned nectarines are especially delicious.

LEMONS
Originally from Southeast Asia, the lemon is now a central element of Mediterranean cooking. The juiciest lemons are fat, thin-skinned and soft to the touch. For dishes that require the zest, use unwaxed lemons.

ORANGES
The first orange introduced to the Mediterranean from Southeast Asia was the bitter Seville orange, but today there are many sweet varieties, including Jaffas and Valencias. Blood oranges provide especially good juice for drinking.

Valencia orange

DRIED FRUIT

The glut of fresh fruit is dried for the winter months, when it is used extensively in savoury and sweet dishes. Apricots, figs, dates, raisins and prunes are particular favourites.

Raisins

Pine kernels

Whole almond

Flaked almonds

Chestnuts

Apricots

Vermilion seeds make a beautiful garnish

Dates

Walnut

NUTS

Pine kernels, taken from pine cones, are the most distinctive nut in the region's cooking; almonds, walnuts, chestnuts, hazelnuts and pistachio nuts are also much used. Shelled nuts should be kept tightly sealed and used quickly. Toasting nuts enhances their flavour.

The flesh of the quince is close-grained

FIGS

A plump, ripe fig has an intensely sweet flavour. Avoid cracked or bruised fruit. Bright green, under-ripe figs are delicious baked.

Juicy white muscat grapes

Black grapes

QUINCES

A relative of the apple and pear, the quince is a hard, acidic fruit and is always eaten cooked, often in the form of a paste. The Moroccans add quinces to tagines.

GRAPES

If there is a definitive Mediterranean fruit, it is the grape, without which there would be no wine. There are myriad species — grown for wine or the table. Look out for tiny black grapes known in Italy as fragoli and muscat grapes.

Watermelon

APPLES

Cultivated originally from the wild crab apple, eating varieties of this fruit vary enormously. Both fresh and dried apples are sometimes added to Moroccan tagines.

MELONS

The yellow-fleshed Charentais, Ogen and Galia melons all give off a powerful fragrance when ripe, so sniff them at the stalk end before buying. A good melon will also feel heavy for its size. Chilled slices of gorgeously coloured watermelon make a refreshing end to a meal.

FISH

The countries of the Mediterranean have always relied heavily for food on the produce of the sea that links them. Today the catches have declined but fish remains a central part of the diet. For me, one of the great pleasures of travel in the area is to sit at a harbourside café, watching the local fishing boats landing their catch.

OTHER TYPICAL FISH
brill, John Dory, hake,
rock fish (the rascasse or scorpion fish,
gurnard, weever and star-gazer), sole,
grouper, bonito, whiting, conger eel

SEA BASS
This firm-fleshed fish is much appreciated for its fine flavour, a fact reflected in its price. Smaller sea bass are best grilled over fennel branches, so the flesh becomes permeated by the aroma, while larger ones have a delicate flavour when poached in a white wine broth.

Smaller sardines
have the best flavour

SARDINES
The sardine is a common catch all over the Mediterranean. It is an inexpensive fish and a valuable source of protein. Very fresh sardines wrapped in vine leaves and grilled over charcoal have a unique flavour.

ANCHOVIES
Most of the anchovies landed are taken to be processed and canned, but this delicate oily fish can sometimes be found fresh in the market.

Fresh anchovies are
delicious deep-fried

FISH STEAKS
For the grill or barbecue, choose firm-fleshed fish that can be cut into steaks or cubes. Swordfish, which is popular in Turkish cuisine, is a good choice, as is tuna, which has been caught in the Mediterranean since classical times. The ugly monkfish is perfect for kebabs.

Swordfish

Monkfish

Tuna

Fresh mackerel
has silvery, green-striped
gleaming skin

MACKEREL
A strongly flavoured fish, mackerel has a high oil content and is particularly suited to being grilled or barbecued. To be enjoyed at its best, mackerel must be especially fresh.

SEA BREAM
There are many varieties of sea bream. The best for eating are dentex, a silver fish with light blue spots, and the gilt-head bream or daurade, a fish distinguished by a golden mark on each cheek. It may be cooked whole or cut into fillets.

RED MULLET
The red mullet is one of the most sought-after Mediterranean fish, valued for its exquisite flavour.

Dentex

GREY MULLET
Growing much larger than the red mullet, the grey mullet is a versatile firm-fleshed fish that is good eaten cold or hot. The roe of the grey mullet is a delicacy used to make Greek taramasalata and Italian bottarga, salted, pressed dried roe encased in wax.

Whitebait

SMALL FISH
All manner of small fry are taken from the Mediterranean to be fried in olive oil and eaten as a snack or first course. Whitebait and the transparent goby are especially popular catches.

SHELLFISH

F reshness is an essential quality of good shellfish. Whenever possible buy fresh raw seafood – translucent pinky grey prawns and freshly gathered live mussels and clams are delectable ingredients, and in the Mediterranean, even crabs and lobsters are sold live.

OTHER TYPICAL SEAFOOD
razor clams, sea urchins, sea snails, date shells (often eaten raw), ormers (similar to abalone), cockles, winkles, whelks

SCALLOPS
In season, the white muscle of the scallop has an orange coral (roe) attached. It should be briefly cooked to retain its succulence.

OYSTERS
Now available all year round due to farming, oysters are delicious both raw and lightly cooked. They must be absolutely fresh.

CLAMS
Of the many species of clams and cockles in the Mediterranean, the tiny Venus clams, or vongole, *are especially sweet and tender.*

Venus clams

Mussels

Large muscle
after cleaning

LOBSTERS
The rock lobster or crawfish, distinguished by its lack of front claws, is more often found in Mediterranean fish markets than the common lobster. It is highly prized for its meaty tail.

Rock lobster

MUSSELS
These vary in size, according to species. Small mussels are particularly sweet. Avoid mussels with broken or cracked shells.

Spider crab

The claws contain
juicy white flesh

CRABS

*The spider crab is named for its long
spindly legs that contain most of the
flesh. It is a popular catch and makes a
dramatic centrepiece to a shellfish platter.
The many different varieties of small crab are
much used in fish soups and stews.*

Squid

CEPHALOPODS

*Squid, cuttlefish and octopus, all of the cephalopod
family, are widely eaten in the Mediterranean.
Small squid and cuttlefish can be quickly
cooked, but larger squid and octopus need slow
cooking, preferably after being marinated to
tenderize the otherwise very chewy flesh.*

Small squid have
tender flesh

Cooked prawn   *Raw prawn*

PRAWNS

*From tiny brown shrimps to fat pink
Mediterranean prawns, there is an
endless variety of these crustaceans.
Separate from this category is the
delectable long-clawed Dublin Bay
prawn or langoustine, which is actually
part of the lobster family. If possible buy
uncooked prawns — they will typically be a
rosy grey, turning pink only when cooked.*

*Dublin Bay
prawn*

MEAT

The dry climate and the small landholdings typical of the Mediterranean have contrived to make meat a rare resource, to be treated as a luxury, and often preserved for times of scarcity. Lamb and pork are more common than beef, and birds of all sorts are eaten. In the cooler months, game is frequently served.

OTHER TYPICAL MEATS
kid (especially popular in Greece), suckling pig, mutton, pheasant, rabbit, hare, wild boar, morcilla (Spanish blood sausage)

DRIED AND CURED MEATS

PANCETTA
The Italian pancetta is the same cut of pork as bacon, cured in salt rather than smoked. The French call this cut petit salé.

Parma ham

Cured ham is typically thinly sliced

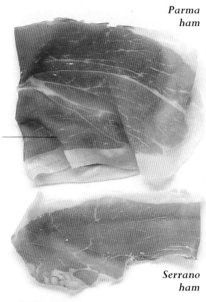

A finely textured salami with relatively high lean meat content

Salami Milano

Serrano ham

CURED RAW HAMS
Whole hams, salted and air-dried, produce delicate meat. The most famous are prosciutto di Parma (Parma ham), *and Spanish* jamón Serrano (Serrano ham).

Salsiccia Calabria

Chorizo

Coarse sausages made from pork and hot spices

CURED SAUSAGES
Best known by their Italian name salami, *there are many types of cured sausages, especially in the western Mediterranean. Usually made with pork, they can be highly spiced or quite mild, intended to be eaten as they are or used in cooking, like the two varieties of Spanish* chorizo.

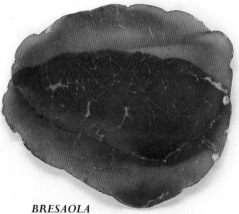

BRESAOLA
This air-dried beef from the southern Alps of Italy is served thinly sliced with olive oil. The Italians also cure meats such as wild boar to ensure a year-round supply.

POULTRY

Barbary duck

Quail

Spring chicken

DUCK
Reared for eggs, meat and liver, ducks and geese are common in the northern Mediterranean. In southern France they are preserved in their fat to make confit. Barbary ducks are a less fatty breed.

SMALL BIRDS
The inhabitants of the Mediterranean are keen hunters and many gamebirds are used in the regional cuisines. Some of the birds, such as pigeons (squabs) and quail, have grown so popular that they are now farmed. Other wild birds that are regularly consumed include partridge, wood pigeon, woodcock, thrush and wild duck. They are valued for their distinctively flavoured lean flesh.

POULTRY
The best chickens are free-range and corn-fed, giving their skin a yellow tinge and making their flesh more flavourful. Mediterranean chickens tend to be killed before they grow very large; the young, small spring chickens (poussins) are excellent for the barbecue. Guinea fowl are also widely reared and turkeys are popular in Italy.

RED MEAT

BEEF
Cattle are difficult to raise in this arid region, although Spain and Italy have popular steak dishes. Beef should be well-hung with an even colour and firm creamy white fat.

LAMB
Lamb has become the most popular red meat in both the eastern and western Mediterranean diet. Mutton is the meat of sheep over a year old; it is darker and has a more pronounced flavour.

VEAL
This tender meat derives from milk-fed beef calves. It should be a light pink in colour. For escalopes, ask your butcher to cut thin slices across the grain and to beat the meat flat.

Merguez

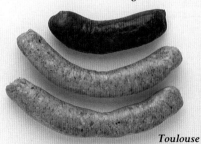

Toulouse sausages

VENISON
A fine-textured dark meat, venison is low in fat and responds well to being marinated before cooking. All animal game is popular in the Mediterranean – rabbit, hare and wild boar are also eaten. Some game animals, such as deer, are farmed to ensure a plentiful supply.

OFFAL
From custom and thrift, no part of an animal is wasted in the Mediterranean, so offal is often served. The kidneys and livers from lambs and veal calves are especially delicious.

SAUSAGES
Mediterranean sausages have a high meat content and are usually made from pork or lamb. Toulouse sausages and spicy lamb Merguez are specialities.

HERBS AND SPICES

Scented bunches of fresh herbs and aromatic spices are one of the delights of the Mediterranean market. With a few exceptions, most herbs are best used fresh. Spices too can easily lose their pungency and should be kept whole in sealed jars and ground as necessary.

OTHER TYPICAL HERBS & SPICES
chervil, marjoram (the cultivated species of oregano), sage, tarragon, caraway seeds, ginger

---

CHIVES
Young chives have a mild onion flavour that complements yogurt- and egg-based dishes.

DILL
Fresh dill is a fragrant salad herb that imparts a delicately aromatic flavour to many cold egg and yogurt dishes.

BAY LEAVES
Used both fresh and dried, bay has a slightly spicy aroma and is often included in stocks, stews and marinades. Bay leaves are best dried on the branch.

DRIED MINT
In the eastern Mediterranean, mint is usually dried for cooking. Moroccans make a refreshing tea from bunches of fresh mint.

NUTMEG
Nutmegs should be kept whole and grated when needed. The lacy outer covering of the nutmeg, mace, is also used in sweet and savoury dishes.

BLACK PEPPERCORNS
Pepper originally came from the Malabar coast of India and is now the most commonly used spice. It should always be freshly ground.

JUNIPER
Berries from the juniper bush are used in marinades for game. Their scent, reminiscent of the gin in which they are a flavouring, is accentuated by crushing.

CLOVES
The dried flower buds of a tropical evergreen, cloves add a warm, spicy note.

CARDAMOM PODS
These seed pods should be crushed to release their full perfumed taste.

FENNEL SEEDS
Toasted fennel seeds have a mild liquorice flavour that is delicious with fish.

THYME
Many varieties of this scrub herb can be found, from tiny creeping plants to bushes. Lemon-scented thyme is particularly aromatic.

Common thyme

Fresh oregano leaves dry well

OREGANO
This popular herb grows wild throughout the Mediterranean. In Greece, *rigani*, as it is known, is often dried to produce a stronger flavour.

ROSEMARY
A robust, spiky-leaved herb with a powerful flavour, rosemary is much used in Italy. It works well in marinades and with roasted and grilled foods.

BASIL
Fragrant, peppery basil is essential to the cooking of southern France and Italy. It blends beautifully with tomatoes. Avoid the dried version.

CORIANDER
Pungently scented coriander is important in many North African and Middle Eastern dishes.

Whole sprigs are best for cooking

PARSLEY
Select the sweet, more powerfully flavoured flat-leaved variety and keep it wrapped in damp newspaper or in a jug of water for freshness.

CINNAMON
Rolled sticks of cinnamon tree bark are used to impart a deep, warm spiciness to meat dishes as well as desserts.

TURMERIC
This vibrant yellow spice is often used to colour dishes in place of saffron, but it has a quite unique, bitter flavour.

CUMIN SEEDS
Commonly used in the east of the region and North Africa, cumin seeds are best kept whole and toasted and ground before using.

SAFFRON
The most expensive spice, saffron is made from the pains-takingly picked stigmas of the *Crocus sativus*. The best saffron comes from La Mancha in Spain.

ALLSPICE
The warmly aromatic allspice berry is used whole and ground in sweets and savouries.

PAPRIKA
Sweet paprika is mildly peppery. It stales quickly so keep it in a tightly sealed jar.

CORIANDER SEEDS
Coriander seeds have a slight orange scent, quite different from the fresh leaves.

STAPLE FOODS

The Mediterranean diet combines relatively low amounts of meat and fish with a pulse or grain to provide bulk. Wheat products, such as pasta, couscous and bread, are especially important; rice is central to both eastern and western Mediterranean cuisine; and high-protein pulses are used with flair in a variety of dishes.

OTHER TYPICAL STAPLE FOODS
black-eyed beans, red kidney beans, cannellini beans, butter beans, split peas, semolina, flour

GRAINS

COUSCOUS
The staple of the North African countries, couscous is a hard wheat semolina grain. It should be steamed over the spicy broth with which it is traditionally served. Pre-cooked couscous is a useful time-saver.

BULGUR WHEAT
This light, nutty-tasting cereal is made up of boiled cracked wheat grains. It needs only to be soaked before use and is essential to Lebanese Tabbouleh (see page 130). It may be finely ground or coarse.

POLENTA
A finely ground maize flour that is popular in northern Italy, polenta is easier to prepare when pre-cooked. It can be served immediately it is cooked or allowed to cool, cut into slices and grilled.

Valencia rice

The fragrant grains stay separate after cooking

Basmati rice

Arborio rice

RICE
It is essential to use the correct rice for a dish as the various grains differ in texture and flavour. For risotto, use short-grain arborio or violone rice; for paella, valencia rice; for eastern Mediterranean dishes, long-grain rices, such as basmati and patna, are excellent.

BREADS

UNLEAVENED BREADS
In the eastern Mediterranean, the usual accompaniment to a meal is a flat, unleavened bread. It stales quickly and so several batches a day are made over a fire or in a charcoal oven. Pitta bread is common, its "pockets" filled with Falafel (see page 72) for the typical Israeli sandwich.

FOCACCIA
Bakers in the Genoese region of Italy pride themselves on their focaccia, an olive oil bread baked in rectangles and topped with rosemary, coarse salt and sometimes slivers of onions. It is usually eaten as a snack.

Unleavened Arab bread

Pitta

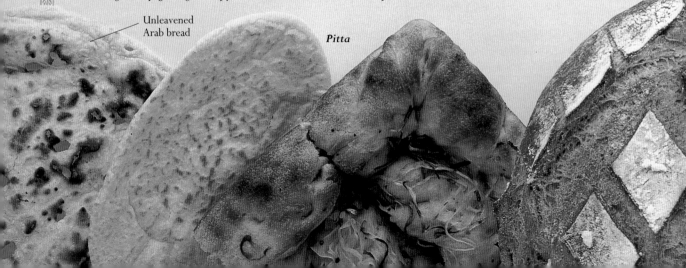

PULSES

BORLOTTI BEANS
Dried borlotti should be soaked overnight and boiled hard for 10 minutes before simmering. They are much used in Italian soups, cook to a creamy consistency and have a high protein content.

BROAD BEANS
Dried broad beans have brown skins and white flesh and are especially popular in Egypt where they are stewed to make Ful Medames (see page 70). They need overnight soaking and long cooking.

CHICK-PEAS
Dried chick-peas that have been soaked overnight then boiled have a rich, nutty flavour and texture that is lacking in canned chick-peas. Chick-pea flour is used in Nice to make the popular bread, socca.

FLAGEOLETS
Pale green flageolet beans have a delicate flavour and a particular affinity with lamb. They are the dried seeds of a dwarf green bean, much used in France.

HARICOT BEANS
Essential for Cassoulet (see page 119), white haricot beans are used in soups, stews and salads. The fresh beans are used in Nice to make Soupe au Pistou (see page 64).

Puy lentils   *Green lentils*

LENTILS
The best lentils are the tiny dark green ones from Le Puy in France. Both Puy and green lentils do not usually need soaking. They provide an excellent foil to rich meat dishes.

PASTA

Spaghetti

Made from durum wheat flour, dried pasta is a high-carbohydrate food that comes in many shapes. It is important to use the correct shape for a particular sauce. Pasta is not restricted to Italy — pasta dishes are also found in Spain and the eastern Mediterranean.

Farfalline: tiny shells for soups

Orecchiette: used to hold sauces

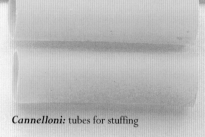

Cannelloni: tubes for stuffing

COUNTRY-STYLE BREADS
Few Mediterranean meals are complete without a basket of robust freshly baked bread. Each region, sometimes each village, has its own distinctive style of bread, using different unrefined flours and distinguished by various flavourings, such as olive oil.

SWEET BREADS
Flavoured sweet breads studded with nuts and fruit, and often glazed with honey and sprinkled with seeds, are particularly common in the western Mediterranean. Many are associated with religious festivals, as with Greek Easter bread or the Christmas bread of Provence.

Olive oil bread

Walnuts are a popular flavouring

Raisin and nut bread

CHEESE AND YOGURT

The aridity of much of the Mediterranean means that cattle are hard to rear and only Italy and France boast a wide range of cheeses made from cow's milk. However, cheeses made from ewe's and goat's milk are common, varying from village to village. Yogurt is widely used, both in savoury dishes or sweetened with fruit and honey.

OTHER TYPICAL CHEESES
Caciocavallo, semi-hard cow's milk cheese (Italy); labneh, made from strained yogurt (Syria and Lebanon); halloumi, ewe's milk cheese (Greece); mascarpone (Italy); Pecorino Romano (Italy); curd cheese

Pyramid-shaped goat's cheese

Herb-covered goat's cheese

Plain goat's cheese

GOAT'S CHEESES
Goat's milk cheeses may be marinated in olive oil, rolled in ash, leaf-wrapped or coated in herbs or pepper. They can be round or cylindrical, tiny or vast blocks, in pyramids or in squares. The flavour varies from mild and creamy to sharp and acidic. Some are very soft and creamy, others hard, depending on their maturity.

Crottin

MANCHEGO
From the La Mancha region of Spain, famous for saffron and Don Quixote, Manchego is found throughout the country and can be recognized by its distinctive black rind. When mature, it hardens and can be grated; try soft young Manchego with quince paste – Dulce de Membrillo (see page 133).

Thick dark rind

DOLCELATTE
This blue cheese from Italy has a mild flavour and creamy texture. Layered with mascarpone, it is known as Torte di Dolcelatte *and makes a very rich after-dinner cheese.*

GORGONZOLA
An Italian cheese, Gorgonzola is made in two strengths — mild, or dolce, and strong, or piccante. It cooks well and makes an excellent pasta sauce when mixed with walnuts. Try serving a slice of Gorgonzola with a very ripe pear.

BANON
Cured in Cognac and wrapped in oak leaves, Banon is a distinctive and delicious goat's cheese from south-west France. Goat's and ewe's milk cheeses are also wrapped in vine and chestnut leaves.

YOGURT
The most flavoursome yogurt is made from ewe's milk. Strained yogurt is good for cooking. Thinned with iced water and sprinkled with herbs, it makes a cooling drink that is popular in the eastern Mediterranean.

Ewe's milk yogurt should be thick and lumpy with a creamy skin

FETA
Salty feta is the favourite cheese of Greece, forming an essential element of the Greek salad. Feta is made from ewe's or goat's cheese and is cured in brine. It should be white and crumbly. Feta does not keep well as it dries out very quickly.

Goat's cheese coated in ash

MOZZARELLA
True mozzarella is made in southern Italy from buffalo's milk. Mozzarella made from cow's milk lacks the smooth texture and subtly sour flavour of the original product.

PECORINO SARDO
From Sardinia, this hard ewe's milk cheese can be used like Parmesan, but is slightly more pungent. It is an essential ingredient of Pesto (see page 42).

A tough-rinded cheese

Look for a pale crumbly surface

RICOTTA
Italian ricotta is a soft cheese made from the whey extracted from cow's milk. It must be eaten very fresh. Its mild creamy flavour makes it particularly suitable for desserts.

PARMESAN
Only cheese stamped Parmigiano-Reggiano is the real thing. Always buy Parmesan in blocks and look for cheese with a grainy quality. Good delicatessens will sell two grades, one for eating as it is and one for grating into dishes.

THE STORECUPBOARD

The storecupboard has always played an important role in the Mediterranean kitchen. The glut of summer produce and the fear of winter scarcity led to a tradition of pickling, preserving and drying so that cooks could enjoy their favourite ingredients all year round.

ADDITIONAL SUPPLIES

Mostardi di frutti (fruits pickled in mustard oil), coffee, rose-water and orange-flower water, sun-dried tomatoes (eaten as an antipasto), gherkins, salt cod

Cep

Horns of plenty

Chanterelles

Bottled pimiento

PICKLES AND PRESERVES

Fruits and vegetables are often preserved for the winter months. Marinated baby artichokes are a delicious antipasto. Bottled red pimiento peppers are much used in Italy and Spain.

DRIED WILD MUSHROOMS

Because of their short season, mushrooms are dried to be reconstituted later in warm water. Look for chanterelles, ceps (porcini), and black horns of plenty (trompettes de mort).

GARLIC

Look for large, firm pink-tinged bulbs, store in a dark place and discard any that start to sprout. Crushing garlic before chopping enhances its flavour. Roasted bulbs are creamy and sweet.

Artichokes in olive oil

Tinned tomatoes

TOMATO PRODUCTS

Tinned plum tomatoes are preferable to under-ripe hot-house tomatoes. The San Marzano variety is best — avoid those with added seasonings. Double concentrate tomato purée thickens and enhances flavour.

Tomato purée

TAHINI PASTE

Made from crushed sesame seeds, tahini is much used in the east of the region. It is sold in glass jars and should be kept in a dark storecupboard or larder.

Red hot chilli paste

HARISSA

This blend of chillies, oil and seasonings accompanies couscous.

PICKLED CAPERS

Capers are the buds of a wild shrub. Those pickled in vinegar should be rinsed before use. Salted capers should be soaked.

Red Wine

Extra-virgin olive oil

Olive oil infused with thyme

Balsamic vinegar

White wine vinegar

OLIVE OIL
This essential ingredient varies in flavour and quality. The better the oil, the lower its acidity. Choose a pungent, deep green, extra-virgin cold-pressed oil for dressings and cold dishes, a standard extra-virgin oil for everyday use, a cheaper olive oil for deep-frying and a herb-scented oil for dressings.

VINEGARS
Wine vinegars and rich, fruity sherry vinegar are much used. Dark, aromatic balsamic vinegar from Modena in Italy is cask-aged, and excellent for dressings.

RED WINE
When cooking with wine, try to find one made in the region from which the dish originates. Fortified wines, such as fino sherry and Marsala, are also useful.

Green olives marinated with lemon and spices

Niçoise olives

OLIVES
Tiny black niçoise olives and marinated green cracked olives are much used in cooking and as antipasti or snacks. Pitted olives are usually inferior in flavour to those with the stone in.

HONEY
The traditional sweetener of ancient Greek and Roman civilizations, honey is used in savoury and sweet dishes. Look for honeys scented with a particular herb or flower, such as lavender.

Coarse flakes can be ground as necessary

ANCHOVIES
Most anchovies are packed in olive oil, but some of the best are packed in salt and should be rinsed well before use. They are particularly widely used in Provençal and Italian cooking.

SEA SALT
This salt has a unique flavour, derived from the different salts in the sea water evaporated to produce it.

CLASSIC
DISHES

The Mediterranean boasts hundreds of classic dishes, the recipes for which are handed down through generations of families. The dishes chosen here, from the sumptuous Italian Zuppa di Pesce to the meze dishes of Turkey and Greece, particularly characterize the region's cooking and should give you a taste for discovering many more traditional specialities. All the dishes serve 4, unless otherwise indicated.

ZUPPA DI PESCE

Italian fish soup

All over the Mediterranean fish soups are made from the day's catch. Each region, indeed each fishing village, has its own variation. This Italian version is more of a stew than a soup. With its tomatoes, wine, olive oil, garlic and delicious fish and shellfish, it encapsulates for me the flavours of the Mediterranean.

INGREDIENTS

1.5kg (3lb) fish (at least 3 of the following: sea bream, red or grey mullet, sardines, mackerel, monkfish, bass, sole)
4 cloves garlic
750g (1½lb) plum tomatoes, skinned and deseeded
3 tbsps chopped fresh parsley
350ml (12fl oz) dry white wine
250g (8oz) small fresh squid
500g (1lb) live mussels and/or live Venus clams
75ml (3fl oz) olive oil
1 onion, chopped
2 dried red chillies, chopped
salt and black pepper
¼ tsp saffron
4 scallops
8 large cooked prawns or raw if available

PREPARATION

1 Remove the fish heads. Place them in a pan with a whole garlic clove, a quarter of the tomatoes, a teaspoon of parsley, a third of the wine and 1.5 litres (2½ pints) of water. Bring to the boil. Simmer for 30 minutes. Strain the resulting stock.

2 Prepare the squid and clean the mussels and clams (see page 153). Cut any fish larger than 15cm (6in) long into 7cm (3in) pieces. Chop the remaining garlic and roughly chop the remainder of the tomatoes.

3 Warm the oil in a pot. Cook the onion until soft, about 20 minutes. Add the garlic and two-thirds of the remaining parsley. Cook for 10 minutes.

4 Add the tomatoes and chillies. Cook for a further 10 minutes, stirring regularly, until the tomatoes have broken down. Pour in the rest of the wine, turn up the heat to bring it to the boil and allow to bubble for 2 minutes. Add the stock, plenty of seasoning and the saffron. Bring to the boil. Reduce the heat and simmer, uncovered, for 15 minutes.

5 Add the fish in order of cooking time: squid, firm fish, whole fish, raw prawns (if using), scallops, cooked prawns and, finally, mussels and clams. The total cooking time should not exceed 20 minutes.

6 Sprinkle with parsley and serve.

Clams

Dry white wine

Parsley

Tomatoes

Garlic

Scallops

Squid

Sea bream

Sardines

Red mullet

ZUPPA DI PESCE

Onion

Red
chillies

Salt

Black
pepper

Saffron

Prawns

Olive oil

Mussels

GAZPACHO ANDALUZ

Andalusian Gazpacho

This soup is essentially a puréed salad, with the refreshing characteristics that description suggests. Spain boasts many different kinds of gazpacho, including an elegant white almond soup, Ajo Blanco con Uvas (see page 60), inherited from the Moors. The soup below is the classic, tomato-rich version – the juicier and riper the tomatoes, the better it will taste.

INGREDIENTS

1kg (2lb) very ripe plum tomatoes, skinned and deseeded
2 green peppers, peeled, cored and deseeded
1 cucumber, peeled
90g (3oz) white bread
½ red onion, chopped
2 cloves garlic, chopped
80ml (2¾fl oz) extra-virgin olive oil
30ml (2 tbsps) sherry vinegar
salt
250ml (8fl oz) iced water

GARNISHES

2 tomatoes
1 green pepper, peeled, cored and deseeded
½ cucumber
1 red onion
2 hard-boiled eggs, peeled
2 slices white bread, crusts removed
olive oil for frying

Red onion

White bread

Cucumber

Green peppers

Tomatoes

PREPARATION

1 Roughly chop the flesh of the tomatoes, reserving the juice. Dice the green peppers. Chop the cucumber. Cut off the bread crusts and tear the bread into small squares.

2 Put the tomatoes and their juice, the peppers, cucumber, onion, garlic, bread, oil and vinegar with some salt and the iced water in a food processor or blender. Blend until the ingredients are well amalgamated, but not too smooth – the soup should have texture.

3 Check the balance of oil and vinegar, adding more of each if necessary. Chill the soup for a minimum of 2–3 hours.

4 Prepare the garnishes. Roughly dice all the vegetables. Coarsely chop the hard-boiled eggs. Cut the bread into small cubes and fry them in olive oil until they turn golden brown on both sides. Arrange the garnishes in small bowls.

5 If desired, thin the soup with more iced water before serving (though it should remain fairly thick). Serve, handing round the garnishes separately.

Garlic

Olive oil

Sherry vinegar

Salt

Hard-boiled
eggs

TAPAS

Tapas, meaning "covers" or "lids", take their name from the little plates of simple appetizers traditionally placed over your glass in a Spanish bar. This selection of some of the slightly more elaborate tapas dishes would be ideal for entertaining.

CHAMPIÑONES AL AJILLO

Mushrooms in garlic

This is the favourite way to prepare mushrooms and works well with cultivated or wild varieties. The mushrooms are sautéed in garlicky olive oil, sprinkled with fresh parsley and finished with a squeeze of lemon.
See page 85 for recipe.

ESPINACAS A LA CATALANA

Spinach Catalan style

The natural sweetness of young spinach is accentuated in this rich dish by pine kernels and plump raisins.
See page 80 for recipe.

PINCHOS MORUNOS

Pork kebabs

These little kebabs are named after the Moorish invaders who first brought spices to Spain. Today they are usually made with pork.
See page 107 for recipe.

SALPICON DE MARISCOS

Shellfish salad

*The key to this dish is the piquant
sauce, spiked with capers and gherkins,
in which the prawns and mussels are
marinated. You can include other shellfish such as clams or winkles, or branch
out with squid, but do not be tempted to
put in the more delicate lobster or crab.*
See page 91 for recipe.

HABAS CON JAMON

Broad beans with ham

*The air-dried ham of Spain rivals in
quality its more famous Italian cousin
from Parma. It has few better partners
than tiny juicy broad beans. The beans
are cooked without water, reflecting the
fact that in parts of Spain water is more
precious than olive oil.*
See page 80 for recipe.

TORTILLA

Potato omelette

*Nothing like the French omelette, the
tortilla is a thick wedge of eggs and
potatoes, at its best when served warm or
cold rather than straight from the pan.
No tapas bar is complete without
tortilla, which is also ideal picnic food.*
See page 85 for recipe.

IMAM BAYILDI
Stuffed aubergine

The Imam swooned when he ate this dish, so the story goes in Turkey, because he found it so delicious. Less romantic historians have suggested he was overcome by the amount of olive oil used in the preparation, but provided the oil is hot enough, the aubergines absorb little of it as they fry. I know which explanation I prefer.

INGREDIENTS

4 medium aubergines
salt
2 green peppers, cored and deseeded
1 large onion
500g (1lb) plum tomatoes, skinned and deseeded
400ml (14fl oz) olive oil
3 cloves garlic, chopped
1 tbsp tomato purée
1 tsp sweet paprika
1 tsp ground allspice
½ tsp black pepper
3 tbsps chopped fresh parsley

PREPARATION

1 Wash the aubergines, leaving the stalks on. With a sharp knife, make a 5cm (2in) deep slit from the stalk to the base, taking care not to cut right through. Sprinkle salt into the slits and leave for 20 minutes.
2 Cut the peppers into fine strips. Peel the onion, cut in half and slice into fine half-moons. Chop the tomatoes into small pieces.
3 Heat a quarter of the oil in a large frying pan over a medium heat. Add the peppers, onion and garlic and fry for 20 minutes, stirring regularly.
4 Preheat the oven to 190°C/375°F/gas 5.
5 Add the tomatoes, tomato purée, spices and half the parsley to the onion and pepper mixture. Cook for a further 10 minutes, stirring regularly.
6 Rinse the aubergines and pat dry. Heat the remaining olive oil and fry the aubergines for 10 minutes, turning several times. Remove, and drain on kitchen paper.
7 Place the aubergines slit side up in an earthenware dish in which they fit snugly. Carefully open the slits and pile in the onion, pepper and tomato mixture. Pour into the dish sufficient boiling water to come halfway up the sides of the aubergines.
8 Bake in the oven for 45 minutes, until very tender. Allow the aubergines to cool in the liquid, then lift out with a slotted spoon. Discard the cooking liquid. Sprinkle with the remaining parsley, and serve.

Tomatoes

Onion

Green peppers

Salt

Aubergines

Olive oil

Garlic

Tomato purée

Sweet paprika

Ground allspice

Black pepper

Parsley

GNOCCHI AL PESTO

Italian potato dumplings with pesto sauce

The classic Italian sauce of pesto combines well with many kinds of pasta, particularly *trenette*, but in its home of Genoa it is traditionally served with potato gnocchi. These little white dumplings are surprisingly light, and form the perfect foil to luscious green basil-scented pesto.

INGREDIENTS

GNOCCHI
750g (1½lb) medium-sized red potatoes
good pinch of salt
175g (6oz) plain flour, plus flour to dust

PESTO
1 large clove garlic
½ tsp salt
60g (2oz) fresh basil
30g (1oz) freshly grated Pecorino Sardo
60g (2oz) freshly grated Parmesan
45g (1½oz) pine kernels
150ml (¼ pint) extra-virgin olive oil

PREPARATION

1 To make the gnocchi, boil the potatoes whole in their skins for 30 minutes or until tender (do not prick to test). Drain, peel, then mash with the salt.
2 Sift the flour then, with your hands, lightly work it into the mashed potato, a tablespoon at a time, until you have a smooth dough.
3 Break the dough in half. Lay one half on a floured surface. Using your palms, roll it out into a long sausage shape. Cut the sausage in half and roll out each half again, until it is about the thickness of your thumb. Repeat with the remaining dough.
4 Flour two baking trays. Cut the dough at 2cm (¾in) intervals. Take a fork and, holding the curved tip towards you, press each piece of dough against the prongs. The gnocchi should be curved, with an indent on one side and ridges on the other to pick up the sauce. Lay them on the trays.
5 To make the pesto, crush the garlic with the salt (see page 150). Tear the basil and, using a pestle and mortar or food processor, combine it with the garlic and salt. Add the cheeses and pine kernels and briefly grind again.
6 Add the oil in a steady trickle, stirring continually or keeping the food processor on, until well blended.
7 Bring a pan of salted water to the boil. Cook the gnocchi in batches – they are done as soon as they rise to the surface (1–2 minutes). Remove with a slotted spoon and place in a warm serving dish. Spoon over the pesto and serve immediately.

Basil

Garlic

Flour

Salt

Potatoes

Pecorino
Sardo

Parmesan

Pine kernels

Olive oil

MEZE

As *tapas* are a way of life in Spain, so are *meze* in the eastern Mediterranean. Here there always seems to be time to enjoy a cup of coffee or a drink with a few little savoury pastries and a selection of freshly made dips. Like tapas, meze make perfect party food.

BABA GHANOUSH

Purée of grilled aubergines

Aubergines grilled until their flesh blackens acquire a new sweetness. In this famous Lebanese dish, the flesh is then mixed with tahini paste and spiked with lemon juice. You can leave the tahini out if you like — then the dish is known as "poor man's caviar".
See page 70 for recipe.

HUMMUS BI TAHINI

Chick-pea and sesame dip

It is hard to imagine a meze table without a plate of hummus, chick-pea purée garnished with spicy red oil and parsley, and served with warm flat bread.
See page 70 for recipe.

TSATSIKI

Yogurt and cucumber dip

When the midday sun blazes down, nothing can be more appetizing than a dish of chilled tsatsiki with fresh bread to scoop up this refreshing yogurt dip.
See page 70 for recipe.

44

BÖREKS

Stuffed savoury pastries

Although the little pastries known in
Turkey as böreks are traditionally made
with watered pastry, a much more
practical alternative is to use ready-
made frozen filo pastry. Feta cheese
crumbled and mixed with chopped dill
makes a deliciously simple filling.
See page 72 for recipe.

FALAFEL

Chick-pea fritters

Falafel are the favourite street food of
Israel, where they are made with chick-
peas (as opposed to the dried broad beans
used in Egypt). They are at their very
best straight from the pan. For a more
complete snack, sandwich them in a
pitta pocket and top with hummus.
See page 72 for recipe.

DOLMATHES

Stuffed vine leaves

Mediterranean cooks make use of all
available ingredients. The vine may be
grown to provide wine, but its leaves are
not allowed to go to waste. Stuffed with
a savoury rice mixture, they become
delectable morsels in their own right.
See page 72 for recipe.

DJEJ EMSHMEL

Tagine of chicken with lemons and olives

Moroccan cuisine is famous for its tagines, delicately spiced casseroles that owe their name to the earthenware pot with its chimney-shaped lid in which they are cooked. This recipe for chicken gently simmered with fat juicy olives and preserved lemons is one of my favourites. Bread is the traditional accompaniment, but Roz bi Saffran (see page 130) complements it perfectly.

Saffron

Ground cumin

Ground cinnamon

Ground ginger

INGREDIENTS

175g (6oz) green cracked olives
1 corn-fed chicken weighing 1.75kg (3½lb)
1 onion
3 cloves garlic, finely chopped
1 tsp black pepper
1 tsp ground ginger
½ tsp ground cinnamon
½ tsp ground cumin
good pinch of saffron
salt
60ml (4 tbsps) olive oil
1 large bunch each of fresh parsley and coriander
2 preserved lemons (see page 133) or 1 fresh lemon
juice of 1 fresh lemon

Black pepper

Garlic

Onion

PREPARATION

1 Cover the olives with water and leave to soak for an hour, changing the water after 30 minutes.
2 Remove any excess fat from the cavity of the chicken, then place it in an oval casserole dish.
3 Grate the flesh of the onion, making sure you catch the juices, and add to the casserole with the garlic, spices, a pinch of salt and the oil.
4 Wash the herbs and set aside sufficient from each bunch to produce 1 tablespoon of chopped leaves. Tie the remainder in a bunch and add to the dish.
5 Pour in just enough water to cover the chicken. Bring to the boil. Reduce the heat and simmer for 30 minutes, turning the chicken after 15 minutes.
6 Drain and rinse the olives. Quarter the preserved lemons and rinse well (or quarter 1 fresh lemon). Add to the dish, together with the olives and lemon juice. Cover and cook for a further 20 minutes.
7 Remove the chicken and wrap in foil. Turn up the heat under the dish and boil rapidly until the sauce is reduced by half. Remove the bunch of herbs and add the fresh chopped leaves. Check the seasoning, adding more salt or lemon juice if required.
8 Cut the chicken into portions and spoon over the spicy sauce. Serve with warm flat bread or fragrant Roz bi Saffran.

Green cracked olives

Chicken

Salt

Olive oil

Parsley

Coriander

Preserved lemons

Fresh lemon
and juice

PISSALADIERE

Provençal onion tart

The classic *pissaladière* is a round bread tart, deeply filled with the delectably sweet onions of the region. This favourite dish of Nice derives its name from the *pissala*, or salt fish paste, with which it was originally smeared. Today it is usually topped with anchovies and olives.

INGREDIENTS

DOUGH
300g (10oz) strong plain flour, plus flour to dust
1 tsp salt
1 tsp white sugar
15g (½oz) dried yeast granules
1 large egg, beaten
30ml (2 tbsps) olive oil

FILLING
1.5kg (3lb) sweet white onions
2 cloves garlic, peeled and lightly crushed
but kept whole
½ tsp salt
45ml (3 tbsps) olive oil
bouquet garni made up of 1 fresh bay leaf and
2 sprigs each of fresh thyme and rosemary
8 anchovy fillets in olive oil
16 small black olives, preferably niçoise

Flour

Salt

White sugar

Dried yeast

Egg

PREPARATION

1 Combine the flour and salt in a heat-proof bowl. Place in a very low oven for 10 minutes.
2 Mix the sugar into 150ml (¼ pint) of warm water and then whisk in the yeast. Cover, and leave to stand for 10 minutes, until frothy.
3 Make a well in the centre of the flour. Add the egg, oil and yeast mixture. Stir together with a wooden spoon, then start to work the dough with floured hands. The mixture will be sticky at first, but after a few minutes will become smooth. Work for a further 5 minutes until pliable.
4 Sprinkle the dough with a little flour. Cover with a cloth, and leave in a warm place for 1 hour, or until doubled in size.
5 Meanwhile, make the filling. Peel the onions, cut in half and slice into fine half-moons. Place in a heavy-lidded pan with the garlic, salt, 15ml (1 tbsp) of oil and the bouquet garni. Cook, covered, over a low heat for 1 hour, stirring occasionally. The onion should be very soft but should remain pale.
6 Preheat the oven to 180°C/350°F/gas 4. Oil a 25cm (10in) tart tin. Knock back the dough (see page 151) and press it out with your hands to fill the tin. Bake in the preheated oven for 10 minutes to dry out the dough. Remove the tin, then turn the oven to its maximum setting.
7 Fill the dough case with the onion, discarding the bouquet garni and garlic. Arrange the anchovies in a lattice over the top of the onion and scatter the olives in between. Pour the remaining oil over the tart. Bake for 15 minutes and serve warm.

Olive oil

Sweet white onions

Garlic

Bouquet garni

Anchovies

Niçoise olives

49

GRILLED FOOD

Throughout the Mediterranean, whether on the shady terrace of a villa or at a street stall, you will find people grilling food over charcoal. It may be meat, fish or vegetables, frequently marinated with a few spices and herbs, and the results are simply served, with bread and perhaps a little freshly made sauce.

DJEJ MESHWI

Grilled spring chicken

In the eastern Mediterranean there are whole restaurants that serve nothing but spring chickens grilled over charcoal. For me, nothing can be more mouth-watering than the sight and smell of these little marinated chickens rotating on the spit.
See page 106 for recipe.

ŞIŞ KÖFTESI

Minced meat on skewers

These skewered minced meat kebabs can fairly be called the hamburger of the eastern Mediterranean. Although they are usually made with lamb, beef can be used if it is not too lean (the fat provides flavour). See page 106 for recipe.

KILIÇ SISTE TARATOR

Swordfish kebabs with walnut sauce

This dish is the pride of the myriad restaurants that line the Bosphorus outside Istanbul. The kebabs of swordfish interspersed with bay leaves sizzle away while you sip your drink and look at the lights of the city across the water.
See page 92 for recipe.

Tarator sauce

PESCE ALLA GRIGLIA SALSA VERDE

Grilled fish with green sauce

Salsa verde, or "green sauce", is deliciously piquant and, being uncooked, very simple to make. In Italy it is traditionally served with boiled meats, but it also makes a perfect accompaniment to grilled fish.
See page 96 for recipe.

Salsa Verde

ŞIŞ KEBABS

Lamb kebabs

This classically simple dish is found all over the eastern Mediterranean. Chunks of lamb are marinated in olive oil and lemon juice and cooked over charcoal for added flavour.
See page 107 for recipe.

PAELLA VALENCIANA

Valencian paella

Taking its name from the *paellera*, a large two-handled shallow pan in which it is prepared, this famous rice dish is traditionally cooked over a wood fire. The people of the Albufera Lake region in Valencia claim to have invented the dish, and the original paella once included rabbit, snails and eels as well as the flat beans for which the area is famous. Today there are many variants of paella – this is one of my favourites. Serves 8.

INGREDIENTS

20 small live clams, such as Venus clams
250g (8oz) long beans, such as runner or flat, trimmed
175g (6oz) plum tomatoes, skinned and deseeded
salt
1 chicken weighing 1.75kg (3½lb),
jointed into 16 pieces (see page 154)
250g (8oz) cooking chorizo
125ml (4fl oz) olive oil
125g (4oz) shelled fresh peas
2 cloves garlic, finely chopped
1 sprig fresh rosemary
1.4 litres (2¼ pints) chicken stock (see page 155)
¼ tsp saffron
500g (1lb) valencia or other short-grained rice,
such as arborio
2 lemons, quartered, to serve

PREPARATION

1 Clean the clams (see page 153). Cut the beans into 3.5cm (1½in) pieces. Roughly chop the tomatoes, being careful not to lose the juices.
2 Sprinkle salt over the chicken pieces. Cut the chorizo into 2.5cm (1in) slices.
3 Heat the oil in a large, deep round pan, preferably a paellera or a wide pan with two handles. The metal of the pan should not be too thick. Add the chicken and the chorizo slices and fry for 5 minutes, turning the pieces from time to time until they are browned on all sides.
4 Add the beans, peas, chopped tomatoes, garlic, rosemary and the stock. Bring to the boil, then add the saffron. Cover and simmer for 10 minutes.
5 Add the rice, and salt to taste. Quickly stir all the ingredients together and bring back to the boil. Cover and leave to simmer for 10 minutes.
6 Remove the lid and add the clams. Cover and leave to cook for a further 10 minutes, until the rice has absorbed all the liquid.
7 Take the pan off the heat, cover it with a clean dry tea towel and leave to stand for 10 minutes before serving with quarters of lemon.

Chorizo

Salt

Tomatoes

Runner beans

Clams

Chicken

Peas

Garlic

Rosemary

Chicken stock

Saffron

Valencia
rice

Lemons

Olive oil

KOUNELLI STIFATHO

Greek rabbit casserole

The ancient Greeks liked to use honey and vinegar to give a sweet and sour touch to their cooking, a habit preserved in this hunters' casserole. Traditionally rabbit or even hare is used, but beef also works well. The real delight of the dish is the rich, spicy red wine sauce studded with baby onions and scented with mountain herbs.

INGREDIENTS

1 large rabbit weighing 1.5kg (3lb), jointed into 8 pieces
flour, to dust
150ml (¼ pint) olive oil
1kg (2lb) small pickling onions
125ml (4fl oz) red wine vinegar
3 cloves garlic, chopped
500g (1lb) plum tomatoes, peeled
1 tbsp ground cumin
1 cinnamon stick
8 allspice berries
8 cloves
1 tbsp clear honey
125g (4oz) tomato purée
600ml (1 pint) robust red wine
salt and black pepper
bouquet garni made up of 2 fresh bay leaves, zest of 1 orange and 3 sprigs each of fresh thyme and oregano

PREPARATION

1 Preheat the oven to 180°C/350°F/gas 4.
2 Dust the rabbit pieces with flour.
3 Heat half the oil in a large heavy frying pan. Add the rabbit pieces and sauté for 5 minutes to brown them. Transfer to a large earthenware casserole.
4 Plunge the onions into boiling water to loosen their skins, remove with a slotted spoon and peel.
5 Turn the heat under the pan to low and add the onions. Cook for 20 minutes, turning them until they are brown all over. Transfer to the casserole.
6 Drain the excess oil from the pan. Turn the heat to medium and add the vinegar and garlic. Cook for 2 minutes, stirring with a wooden spoon.
7 Add the tomatoes, spices and honey to the pan. Cook for 5 minutes, then stir in the tomato purée, red wine and remaining oil. Bring to the boil, season generously, and pour into the casserole.
8 Tuck the bouquet garni into the casserole, leaving the string outside for easy removal.
9 Cover the casserole and place in the oven. Bake for 30 minutes. Reduce the heat to 150°C/300°F/gas 2 and bake for 1½ hours. Check the seasoning, remove the bouquet garni and cinnamon, and serve.

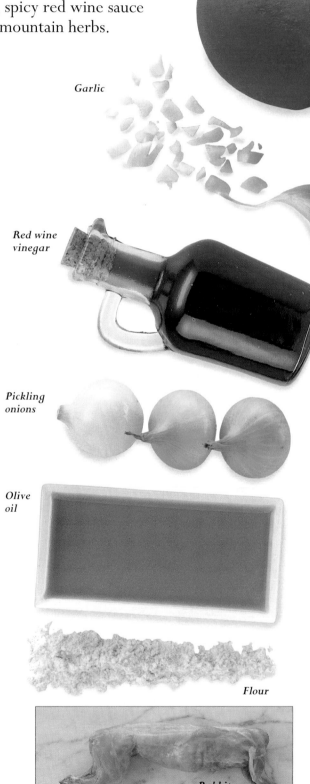

Garlic

Red wine vinegar

Pickling onions

Olive oil

Flour

Rabbit

Cloves

Allspice
berries

Clear
honey

Tomato
purée

Red wine

Salt

Black
pepper

Bouquet
garni

Ground
cumin

Cinnamon
stick

Tomatoes

ROUGETS A LA NIÇOISE

Red mullet Niçois style

For me, red mullet are the quintessential fish of the Mediterranean. On my honeymoon in Turkey, spent aboard a little fishing boat, we bought some straight from the fishermen and fried them there and then in olive oil. That remains a most delicious memory. This equally simple but delectable dish from Nice uses just about every classic ingredient of the region.

INGREDIENTS

8 small red mullet weighing 175–250g (6–8oz) each
or 4 large red mullet weighing 375–425g
(12–14oz) each
125ml (4fl oz) olive oil
1 onion, finely chopped
3 cloves garlic, finely chopped
3 tbsps chopped fresh parsley
1 tsp tomato purée
60ml (4 tbsps) dry white wine
1kg (2lb) plum tomatoes, skinned and chopped
salt and black pepper
flour, to dust
125g (4oz) small black olives, preferably niçoise
4 tbsps capers, rinsed and drained
16 anchovy fillets in olive oil
2 lemons, sliced

PREPARATION

1 Scale and gut the mullet (see page 150). If you like a slightly gamey taste, leave in the liver (this is traditional in Nice). Preheat the oven to 180°C/350°F/gas 4.
2 Heat 60ml (4 tbsps) of oil and fry the onion over a medium heat, stirring regularly, until golden. Add the garlic and almost all the parsley, reserving a little for a garnish, and fry for another 5 minutes.
3 Stir the tomato purée into the white wine. Add the tomatoes, tomato purée and wine mixture and seasoning to the pan. Simmer uncovered for 15 minutes, stirring occasionally to help the tomatoes break down, until you have a thick tomato sauce.
4 Season the flour and lightly dust the mullet.
5 Warm the remaining oil over a high heat in a non-stick frying pan in which the fish lie flat. When the oil is very hot, add the fish. Fry for 4 minutes on each side, then remove with a slotted spoon.
6 Arrange the mullet in a single layer in an earthenware dish, then pour over the tomato sauce. Arrange the olives, capers, anchovies and lemon slices over the top. Place in the preheated oven and bake for 15–20 minutes. Serve the fish piping hot, straight from the dish.

White wine

Tomato purée

Parsley

Garlic

Onion

Olive oil

Red mullet

Black
pepper

Salt

Flour

Niçoise
olives

Capers

Anchovies

Lemons

Tomatoes

RECIPES

The countries that range around the Mediterranean Sea may follow the same basic principles in the kitchen, but they also offer a wealth of regional variety. This recipe collection reflects that rich diversity. Here you will find a delicate chilled white soup from Andalusia and a warming minestrone from Livorno, a spicy tagine from Fez, a herb-scented Provençal daube and sardines barbecued Turkish style. An inspirational menu planner will also help you to assemble memorable meals, from a leisurely lunch for a summer's day to a delicately spiced North African feast. All the dishes serve 4, unless otherwise indicated.

SOUPS

Mediterranean food has its roots in a peasant culture, and soups are the ultimate peasant fare. Several of those featured here are sufficiently substantial to serve as main courses. Try a real Minestrone, so thick you can stand your spoon up in it, the basil-scented Soupe au Pistou of Provence, or Harira, the spicy Moroccan soup traditionally served as dusk falls during Ramadan. For hotter days, look to the lighter, elegant chilled soups, such as the garlicky white version of gazpacho found in Andalusia or the simple cucumber and yogurt soup of Turkey.

AJO BLANCO CON UVAS

Iced almond soup with grapes

Known as "white gazpacho", this soup is believed to have been introduced to Andalusia by the Moors, who certainly brought the almond trees that yield the central ingredient. The thick garlicky white liquid, studded with grapes, should be served very cold.

INGREDIENTS

125g (4oz) blanched almonds, coarsely chopped
3 cloves garlic
½ tsp salt
4 slices day-old white bread, crusts removed
250g (8oz) seedless white grapes
90ml (3fl oz) extra-virgin olive oil
30ml (2 tbsps) white wine vinegar
900ml (1½ pints) iced water

PREPARATION

1 Grind the chopped almonds, garlic and salt to a fine paste. (Traditionally this stage is done with a pestle and mortar, but a food processor can also be used successfully.)
2 Soak the bread for 5 minutes in a little cold water, then squeeze it dry. Add the bread to the almond and garlic paste, then grind or process again until smooth.
3 Pour boiling water over the grapes to loosen the skins, then drain and peel them.
4 Very slowly beat the oil into the almond, garlic and bread paste, followed by the wine vinegar.
5 Pour in the iced water, check for salt, and place the soup in the refrigerator to chill thoroughly.
6 Just before serving garnish the chilled soup with the peeled grapes.

ÇAÇIK SOUPA

Cold soup of yogurt and cucumber

Çaçik (or tsatsiki as it is known in Greece), the traditional Turkish meze of yogurt and cucumber, can also be served in soup form when thinned with iced water. Studded with pale green cucumber and flecked with bright green dill, this soup makes a refreshing starter on a hot day.

INGREDIENTS

1½ small cucumbers, peeled
salt
750ml (1¼ pints) strained natural yogurt
juice of ½ lemon
30ml (2 tbsps) olive oil
½ clove garlic, crushed and chopped
250ml (8fl oz) iced water
4 tbsps finely chopped fresh dill

PREPARATION

1 Coarsely grate the cucumbers using a food processor or grater. Place in a bowl, sprinkle well with salt and leave to stand for 15 minutes.
2 Beat the yogurt with the lemon juice, oil, garlic and iced water. If necessary, add a little more water to thin the mixture, but the finished soup should be quite thick.
3 Rinse the cucumber, pat dry with kitchen towels and add to the yogurt mixture. Stir in the dill, reserving a little for a garnish. Chill well and garnish with the remaining dill before serving.

VARIATION

• Use a mixture of half fresh dill and half fresh mint to flavour the soup and replace a quarter of the yogurt with soured cream.

SOUPE DE POTIRON

Pumpkin soup

This deep yellow soup from Provence is enormously comforting on a cool evening. Choose small sweet pumpkins rather than overgrown ones, which are best kept for Hallowe'en. Serves 6–8.

INGREDIENTS

1.75kg (3½lb) pumpkin
3 white onions
1 clove garlic, finely chopped
2 fresh sage leaves
30ml (2 tbsps) olive oil
salt and black pepper
90g (3oz) long-grain rice, rinsed and drained
shavings of fresh Parmesan, to serve

PREPARATION

1 Peel the pumpkin and cut the flesh into 2.5cm (1in) cubes. Peel the onions, cut in half and slice into fine half-moons.
2 Place the pumpkin, onion and garlic in a large heavy pan with the sage leaves and oil. Pour over 2.5 litres (4 pints) of boiling water. Add seasoning to taste and simmer slowly for 45 minutes.
3 Purée the soup in a blender or food processor.
4 Return the soup to the pan and bring back to the boil. Add the rice to the pan and cook for 15 minutes, until soft. Check the seasoning, then garnish with Parmesan.

VARIATION

• Replace the rice with 90g (3oz) vermicelli, broken up and cooked in the soup for 10 minutes.

MINESTRONE ALLA LIVORNESE

Vegetable soup Livorno style

There is no definitive recipe for minestrone, or "big soup" as it is translated. Each region, each village, each family in Italy has its own recipe, and varies the vegetables according to the season. This is a cold-weather version from Livorno. Serves 6–8.

INGREDIENTS

125g (4oz) pancetta, diced
2 onions, finely chopped
2 cloves garlic, finely chopped
30ml (2 tbsps) extra-virgin olive oil
500g (1lb) plum tomatoes, skinned, deseeded and chopped
125g (4oz) Parma ham, cut into strips
bouquet garni made up of 1 fresh bay leaf and 2 sprigs each of fresh parsley, thyme and rosemary
125g (4oz) dried borlotti beans, soaked overnight
1.5kg (3lb) mixed vegetables, such as carrots, cauliflower, savoy cabbage, leeks, celery, potatoes, pumpkin
salt and black pepper
extra-virgin olive oil and freshly grated Parmesan, to serve

PREPARATION

1 Place a large heavy pan over a medium heat. Put the pancetta, onion, garlic and olive oil in the pan and cook for 10 minutes, stirring frequently.
2 Add the tomatoes and cook for a further 5 minutes, until they have broken down.
3 Stir in the Parma ham, the bouquet garni, the beans and 2 litres (3½ pints) of water and bring to the boil. Reduce to a simmer, cover and leave to cook for 1 hour, or until the beans are tender.
4 Meanwhile prepare the vegetables, peeling and dicing them, where necessary, cutting cabbage into thin strips and leeks into thin rounds.
5 After the soup has cooked for 1 hour, add the vegetables. Check the broth for saltiness and season. Leave to simmer for 30 minutes, or until the vegetables are tender. Discard the bouquet garni.
6 Serve the minestrone with a little jug of extra-virgin olive oil and plenty of Parmesan.

VARIATIONS

• Add 90g (3oz) *tubetti*, or other small pasta, 15 minutes before the end of cooking time.
• Make a summery Genoese green minestrone, with a mixture of leeks, green beans, Swiss chard, courgettes and cannellini beans. Garnish it with basil leaves or with a tablespoon of freshly made Pesto (see page 42).

Bouquet garni

Parma ham

Tomatoes

Olive oil

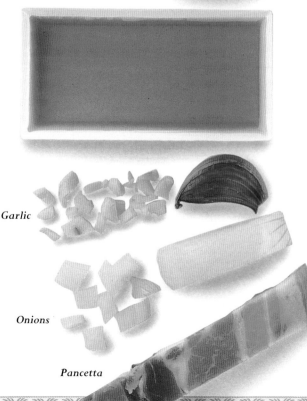

Garlic

Onions

Pancetta

Dried borlotti
beans

Carrots

Cauliflower

Savoy
cabbage

Leeks

Salt

Black
pepper

Parmesan

SOUPE AU PISTOU
Vegetable soup with pistou sauce

Genoa has pesto, Nice has pistou, without the pine kernels. In the early summer months, both cities prepare a delectable green vegetable soup, finished with their own famous sauce.

INGREDIENTS

2 young leeks
90ml (3fl oz) olive oil
6 cloves garlic
375g (12oz) plum tomatoes, skinned, deseeded and chopped
250g (8oz) small courgettes
250g (8oz) French string beans or green beans
175g (6oz) Swiss chard tops, thoroughly washed
salt and black pepper
bouquet garni made up of 2 sprigs each of fresh parsley, sage and basil
250g (8oz) shelled fresh haricot beans or broad beans
90g (3oz) vermicelli
60g (2oz) fresh basil leaves, torn
60g (2oz) freshly grated Parmesan

PREPARATION

1 Remove the green ends of the leeks and chop the white parts finely. Heat 30ml (2 tbsps) of oil in a heavy pan over a low heat and add the leeks and 2 cloves of garlic, finely chopped. Sweat for 10 minutes, until softened, then add the tomatoes. Cook gently for a further 5 minutes, until the tomatoes have broken down.
2 Meanwhile dice the courgettes and cut the French beans into 2.5cm (1in) lengths and cut the Swiss chard tops into strips. When the tomatoes have broken down, add these vegetables to the pan, together with 2 litres (3½ pints) of boiling water, some seasoning and the bouquet garni. Bring back to the boil and simmer for 25 minutes.
3 Add the haricot beans and vermicelli to the pan. Leave to cook for 10–15 minutes.
4 Prepare the pistou. First pound the remaining garlic with a good pinch of salt (this should be done with a pestle and mortar for best results). When the garlic has become a paste, add the basil leaves. Pound again until you have a smooth green paste then, with a fork, incorporate the Parmesan. Finally, stir in the remaining olive oil.
5 Remove the soup from the heat and check the balance of seasoning. Discard the bouquet garni. Stir in the pistou just before serving (once the pistou has been added, do not reheat the soup).

HARIRA
Ramadan soup

Each night of the Muslim month of Ramadan in Morocco, steaming cauldrons of harira await the faithful. The spicy, herb-laden soup rewards those who have fasted during the long daylight hours. This dish serves 6–8.

INGREDIENTS

175g (6oz) dried chick-peas, soaked overnight
1 chicken carcass or 500g (1lb) lamb bones
1 large bunch fresh coriander, plus 3 tbsps chopped fresh coriander
1 large bunch fresh parsley, plus 3 tbsps chopped fresh parsley
125g (4oz) yellow lentils
1 tsp turmeric
2 tsps ground cinnamon
1 tsp ground ginger
1 tsp ground cumin
1 tsp black pepper
salt
2 mild white onions
500g (1lb) plum tomatoes, skinned, deseeded and chopped
1 tsp tomato purée
2 tbsps plain flour
30ml (2 tbsps) olive oil
juice of 1 lemon
1 whole unwaxed lemon, cut into wedges
6–8 tsps harissa, to serve (see page 30)

PREPARATION

1 Drain the chick-peas and put them in a large pan with the chicken carcass, the bunches of herbs tied together and 2.5 litres (4 pints) of water. Bring to the boil, cover and simmer for 1 hour, or until the chick-peas are soft. Remove the chicken carcass and the bunches of herbs, and discard.
2 Add the lentils, spices and salt to the pan. Cover, then simmer for a further 20 minutes.
3 Grate the onions, being careful not to lose the juices. Add the chopped tomatoes, tomato purée and the onion and simmer gently for 30 minutes, stirring occasionally.
4 Beat the flour into 150ml (¼ pint) of cold water, making sure that there are no lumps in the final mixture. Fifteen minutes before serving, stir the flour and water mix into the harira. Cook uncovered for a further 10 minutes, stirring continuously, until the soup has thickened.
5 Pour in the olive oil and lemon juice and sprinkle in the chopped parsley and coriander. Cook gently for another 2–3 minutes. Garnish each serving with a lemon wedge and a teaspoon of fiery harissa.

SOUPE AUX MOULES
Mussel soup

This is a delicate yellow broth made from the
cooking liquid of mussels, studded with vermicelli and
small sweet orange mussels, and flecked with basil.
It looks as good as it tastes.

INGREDIENTS
2kg (4lb) live mussels
bouquet garni made up of 1 fresh bay leaf and 2 sprigs
each of fresh parsley, thyme and fennel
2 litres (3½ pints) shellfish stock (see page 155) or water
45ml (3 tbsps) olive oil
1 onion, chopped
2 cloves garlic, finely chopped
500g (1lb) plum tomatoes, skinned, deseeded
and chopped
good pinch of saffron
90g (3oz) vermicelli, broken up
salt and black pepper
good handful of basil leaves, torn
juice of ½ lemon

PREPARATION
1 Clean the mussels (see page 153). Place the
bouquet garni in the stock or water and bring to
the boil. Add the mussels. Cook for 4 minutes,
shaking the pan occasionally, until the mussels have
opened. Pour the liquid into a bowl, discarding the
bouquet garni, and leave the mussels to cool.
2 Heat the oil in a heavy pan large enough to hold
the mussel liquid. Add the onion and garlic and fry
gently for 10 minutes.
3 Add the tomatoes. Fry for a further 5
minutes over a gentle heat, stirring
occasionally, until the tomatoes have broken down.
4 Strain the mussel liquid through muslin to
remove any grit, then pour it into the pan with the
tomato mixture and bring to the boil.
5 Add the saffron, vermicelli and the seasoning
(be careful with the salt as the mussel liquid will
already be quite salty). Simmer, uncovered, for
10–15 minutes, until the vermicelli is cooked.
6 Meanwhile, pick the mussels out of their shells,
discarding any shells that have failed to open.
Take the pan off the heat and stir in the torn
basil leaves and the cooked mussels.
7 Finish the soup with a squeeze of lemon and
serve immediately. Do not bring the soup back to
the boil or the mussels will toughen.

VARIATION
• Replace the basil leaves with 2 tablespoons of
freshly made Pesto (see page 42).

AVGOLEMONO SOUPA
Chicken soup with eggs and lemon

This simple Greek soup of chicken broth with rice is
made special by the last-minute addition of eggs to
enrich and thicken, and lemon juice to give sharpness.
The result is both refreshing and nourishing.

INGREDIENTS
1.5 litres (2½ pints) chicken stock (see page 155)
45g (1½oz) long-grain rice, rinsed and drained
salt
2 large eggs, plus 1 egg yolk
juice of 1 lemon

PREPARATION
1 Bring the stock to the boil. Add the rice to the
stock together with a good pinch of salt. Boil
uncovered for 10–15 minutes, until the rice is
cooked through.
2 Beat together the whole eggs, the egg yolk and
the lemon juice. Add 60ml (4 tbsps) of the hot
stock to this mixture and rapidly whisk together
until thoroughly combined and smooth.
3 Take the soup off the heat and whisk in the egg
and lemon mixture, being careful not to let it
curdle. Beat for 2 minutes, until you have a slightly
thickened, creamy soup.

FIRST COURSES AND SNACKS

The people of the Mediterranean are hospitable, and rarely offer a glass of wine without a little dish of delicacies to nibble at. Whether it is *tapas* in Spain, *meze* in Greece and Turkey or *antipasti* in Italy, there is a vast selection of light appetizers to choose from. Many Mediterranean dips and spreads for bread are ideal for drinks parties as well as first courses. For more substantial snacks, try Pan Bagnat or Mozzarella in Carrozza, a deep-fried cheese sandwich originating from the south of Italy.

ALLIOLI

Garlic and olive oil sauce

The Catalans make allioli *with nothing but garlic and olive oil and scorn the Provençals up the coast who use egg yolks to help bind the emulsion. Allioli can simply be spread on bread, but is especially good served as a dip with a selection of raw, sliced vegetables.*

INGREDIENTS

6 fat cloves garlic
1 tsp salt
175ml (6fl oz) extra-virgin olive oil

PREPARATION

1 Make sure all the ingredients are at room temperature. Crush the garlic and the salt using a pestle and mortar until you have a smooth paste.
2 Add just a drop of oil to the paste and continue to pound until it has been thoroughly incorporated.
3 Continue to add the oil drop by drop, pounding all the time, until an emulsion begins to form (see page 156). If you add the oil too quickly, the mixture will not emulsify. Conversely, once you have achieved a thick emulsion, stop adding oil at once or you will "break" the emulsification. This sauce should not be chilled before serving.

VARIATIONS

• Add 2 egg yolks (making sure they are at room temperature) to the garlic paste in the mortar. This makes the sauce much easier to blend. Make sure you use very fresh eggs.
• Add 1 tablespoon of fresh white breadcrumbs to the garlic paste to help the sauce to thicken.

TAPENADE

Olive and caper paste

Every cook in Provence has a family recipe for this powerfully flavoured spread. Preserved tuna and anchovies are sometimes included, the herbs and spices vary, but the essentials are the small black olives of the region and the pickled buds from the caper bush.

INGREDIENTS

125g (4oz) capers, preferably packed in salt
250g (8oz) pitted small black olives, preferably niçoise
good pinch of dried thyme
½ dried bay leaf, crumbled
1 clove, ground
salt and black pepper
125ml (4fl oz) extra-virgin olive oil
squeeze of fresh lemon juice
1 baguette

PREPARATION

1 Soak capers preserved in salt in water for 1 hour, changing the water halfway through (capers in vinegar require only 20 minutes soaking). Drain the capers and dry on kitchen paper.
2 Place the capers in a food processor with the remaining ingredients, except the baguette, and blend to a smooth paste.
3 Slice the baguette into 1.5cm (¾in) pieces. Toast both sides until golden brown, spread one side with the paste and serve. Any remaining tapenade will keep for several days in the refrigerator if covered with a thin film of oil.

VARIATION

• Spread tapenade on halved hard-boiled eggs.

ANCHOÏADE

Anchovy paste

The people of the South of France are addicted to anchovies and for centuries have preserved the catch in vast barrels of salt to make sure that they can have a continual supply of them.

INGREDIENTS

100g (3½oz) anchovy fillets, preferably packed in salt
2 cloves garlic
black pepper
60ml (4 tbsps) olive oil
15ml (1 tbsp) red wine vinegar
1 baguette

PREPARATION

1 Drain the salted anchovies and soak them in water for 10 minutes to remove excess saltiness (this is not necessary if using anchovies in olive oil).
2 Crush the garlic using a pestle and mortar, then add the anchovies and a good pinch of pepper, and pound to a paste (this can also be done in a food processor, though with less satisfactory results).
3 Slowly add the oil, pounding continually or keeping the food processor on until the mixture emulsifies. Finally, stir in the vinegar.
4 Slice the baguette and toast. Spread the slices with the salty paste.

VARIATION

• To make a simple hors d'oeuvre, spread anchoïade on quarters of ripe tomatoes and hard-boiled eggs.

DUKKAH

Egyptian roasted spice and nut mix

Even if you could only afford the simplest dinner of bread and oil, a little pile of this spicy mix would make your meal enjoyable. Make it in large amounts and store in airtight containers. Serve it as a dip with bread and fruity olive oil.

INGREDIENTS

100g (3½oz) sesame seeds
30g (1oz) cumin seeds
45g (1½oz) coriander seeds
60g (2oz) shelled, skinned hazelnuts
60g (2oz) roasted chick-peas, optional
1 tsp salt
½ tsp black pepper

PREPARATION

1 Place a heavy frying pan over a moderate heat. When the pan is hot, add the sesame seeds and stir constantly until they are lightly browned all over – take care that they do not burn.
2 Set the sesame seeds aside to cool. In the same pan, toast the cumin seeds until lightly browned and the coriander seeds until they start to pop. Toast the hazelnuts until browned all over. Leave to cool.
3 Mix together the seeds, nuts and chick-peas, if using, with the salt and pepper. Pour the mixture into a food processor or coffee grinder and grind until you have a dry powdery mix.

PAN BAGNAT

Salade niçoise in a roll

Pan bagnat *literally means "wet bread". Originally it was simply a salade niçoise to which stale bread had been added, weighted down and left to absorb the delicious juice of the tomatoes and the deep green olive oil. But the salad was such a favourite mid-morning snack with farm workers that it was soon served in rolls, so that it could easily be carried into the fields and vineyards. I can't think of anything better for a picnic on a sunny day.*

INGREDIENTS

6 large ripe plum tomatoes, quartered
salt
1 large cucumber
2 green peppers, halved and cored
1 red onion
250g (8oz) shelled baby broad beans
3 hard-boiled eggs
250g (8oz) tuna in olive oil
60g (2oz) anchovy fillets, preferably packed in salt
4 large round country bread rolls, such as ciabatta
1 clove garlic
15ml (1 tbsp) red wine vinegar
30ml (2 tbsps) olive oil
125g (4oz) small black olives, preferably niçoise
good handful of basil leaves, torn
black pepper

PREPARATION

1 Sprinkle the tomatoes with salt and leave to stand for 10 minutes.
2 Using a potato peeler, remove the skin of the cucumber and peppers. Finely slice the cucumber and cut the pepper into thin strips. Peel the onion, cut in half and slice into fine half-moons.
3 Blanch the broad beans for 1 minute in boiling water, then slip off the tough outer skins.
4 Peel the hard-boiled eggs and cut into quarters.
5 Drain the tuna. Drain the anchovies and soak them in water for 10 minutes to remove excess saltiness (this is not necessary if using anchovies in olive oil). Reserve two anchovies and chop the rest.
6 Rinse the tomatoes. Mix together the cucumber, peppers, onion and broad beans.
7 Cut the rolls in half. Scoop out the dough to make eight bread shells. Cut the garlic clove in half and rub the insides of the bread shells with the cut side. Sprinkle with vinegar and olive oil.
8 Pile in the vegetable mixture, arrange the tomatoes and eggs on top and scatter over the tuna and olives. Sprinkle with shredded basil leaves and pepper. Finish with half an anchovy.

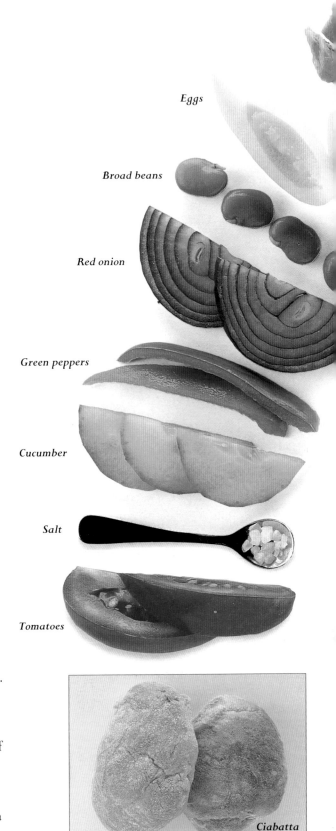

Eggs

Broad beans

Red onion

Green peppers

Cucumber

Salt

Tomatoes

Ciabatta rolls

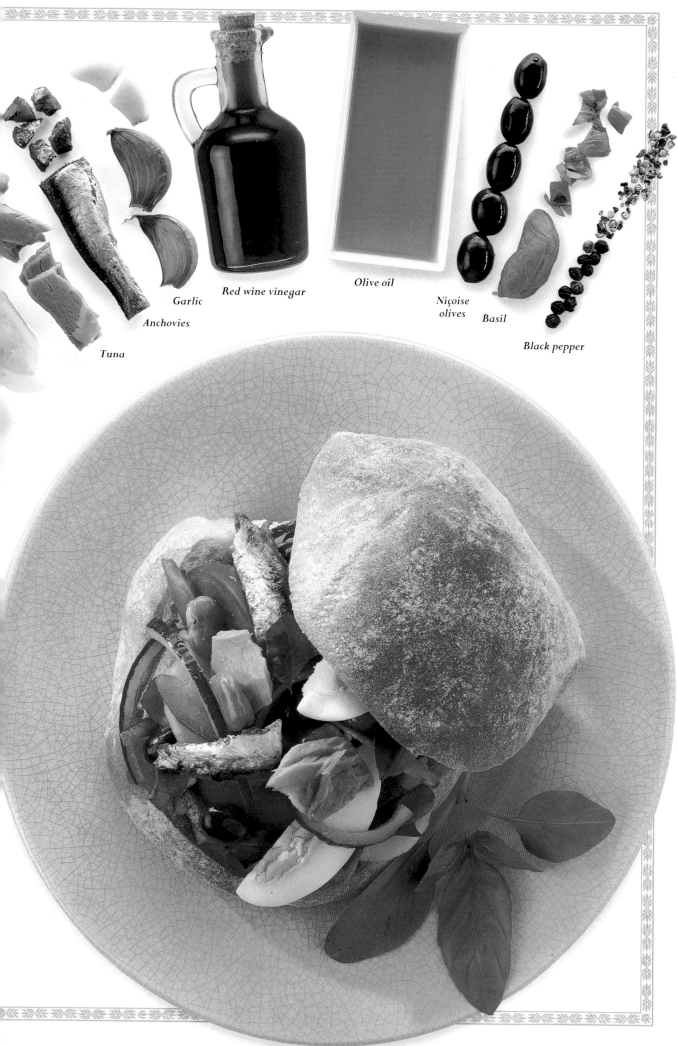

Tuna

Anchovies

Garlic

Red wine vinegar

Olive oil

Niçoise olives

Basil

Black pepper

BABA GHANOUSH

Lebanese purée of grilled aubergines

Illustrated on page 44.

INGREDIENTS

3 large aubergines
2 cloves garlic, crushed
juice of 3 lemons
150ml (¼ pint) tahini paste
salt
1 tsp ground cumin
6 black olives

PREPARATION

1 Grill the aubergines under a hot grill for 20 minutes, turning them regularly until the skin is blackened and blistered all over. Cover with a clean tea towel for 10 minutes then peel off the skin. Squeeze the juice out of the aubergine flesh.
2 Using a food processor or blender, purée the aubergine flesh with the garlic, lemon juice, tahini, salt and cumin. Check the balance of flavours – you may need to add more lemon juice or salt. Garnish with olives and serve.

HUMMUS BI TAHINI

Chick-pea and sesame dip

Illustrated on page 44.

INGREDIENTS

175g (6oz) dried chick-peas, soaked overnight
juice of 2 lemons
150ml (¼ pint) tahini paste
2 cloves garlic
salt
1 tsp sweet paprika
30ml (2 tbsps) olive oil
1 tbsp chopped fresh parsley

PREPARATION

1 Bring a large pan of water to the boil and add the drained chick-peas. Boil for 10 minutes, then reduce the heat and simmer for 1½ hours, until the chick-peas are very soft.
2 Using a food processor, purée the chick-peas with the lemon juice, tahini, garlic and salt to taste. The result should be a smooth, slightly grainy paste. Check the balance of lemon juice and salt.
3 Arrange the hummus in a small bowl or on a plate. Just before serving, mix the paprika into the oil and dribble it over the hummus in a swirl. Finally, sprinkle with the chopped parsley.

TSATSIKI

Greek yogurt and cucumber dip

Illustrated on page 44.

INGREDIENTS

2 small cucumbers, peeled and diced
salt
2 cloves garlic
600ml (1 pint) thick natural yogurt, preferably ewe's or goat's milk
2 tsps dried mint

PREPARATION

1 Place the cucumber in a colander and sprinkle generously with salt. Leave to drain for 45 minutes, then rinse and pat dry with kitchen paper.
2 Using a pestle and mortar, or a teaspoon, crush the garlic with a little salt.
3 Mix the garlic into the yogurt, followed by the mint. Finally add the cucumber. Chill well.

FUL MEDAMES

Stewed beans

The traditional Egyptian breakfast, Ful Medames is something of an acquired taste first thing in the morning, given its pungent flavourings. But it makes a simple, comforting snack at other times of the day.

INGREDIENTS

300g (10oz) dried Egyptian brown beans or broad beans, soaked overnight
salt
GARNISHES
olive oil
3 lemons, quartered
2 cloves garlic, crushed and chopped
4 tsps ground cumin
4 tbsps chopped fresh parsley

PREPARATION

1 Bring twice the volume of water to beans to the boil and add the beans. Simmer for 1½–2 hours, until the beans are soft, but not falling apart – the exact time will depend on the size and age of the beans. Add salt and a little boiling water, if needed, at the end, but do not make the mixture too soupy.
2 Put the garnishes in small bowls so that diners can season to their taste.

VARIATION

• Serve with quartered hard-boiled eggs and sliced tomatoes and red onions.

MOZZARELLA IN CARROZZA

Deep-fried mozzarella sandwiches

The Neapolitans claim as their own this snack of mozzarella in its bread "carriage", alluding to the famous carriages of Naples that once crisscrossed the old city.

INGREDIENTS

200g (7oz) mozzarella (drained weight)
8 thin slices day-old white country-style bread,
crusts removed
125ml (4fl oz) full-cream milk
4 anchovy fillets
black pepper
4 tbsps plain flour
2 eggs, beaten
oil for deep-frying, preferably olive oil

PREPARATION

1 Cut the mozzarella into 4 slices approximately 1cm (½ in) thick. Trim the bread slices so they are 2.5cm (1in) bigger all round than a slice of cheese.
2 Dip one side of each piece of bread into the milk. Lay a slice of mozzarella on the dry side of the bread, drape an anchovy over it, add plenty of pepper and lay another piece of bread on top, dry-side down. Press the edges of the sandwich together so that they are sealed. Repeat this process with the remaining slices of bread and mozzarella.
3 Dip each sandwich in flour and then in the beaten egg, making sure it is well coated.
4 Pour oil to a depth of 2.5cm (1 in) into a pan large enough to hold all 4 sandwiches, and heat. When the oil is hot (when a cube of bread dropped in it turns golden) add the sandwiches. Fry until crisp, turning once, and drain on kitchen paper. Serve hot.

BRIK A L'OEUF

Fried pastries with egg and tuna

This Tunisian snack is fiddly to prepare, but it's worth the effort when you bite into the crisp pastry to find lightly cooked egg yolk.

INGREDIENTS

30ml (2 tbsps) olive oil
2 onions, finely chopped
250g (8oz) tuna in olive oil
salt
good pinch of cayenne pepper
4 tbsps finely chopped fresh parsley
sunflower or vegetable oil for frying
6 sheets filo pastry
4 small eggs

PREPARATION

1 Heat the olive oil and fry the onion over a gentle heat for 10 minutes, until soft. Drain the tuna and mash it with a fork. Combine the softened onions, tuna, salt, cayenne pepper and parsley.
2 Pour sunflower or vegetable oil to a depth of 2.5cm (1in) into a deep frying pan and heat gently.
3 Cut two sheets of pastry in half. Lay out a sheet of pastry and place a half sheet across one end. Keep the remaining pastry covered with a damp tea towel.
4 Place 2 tablespoons of tuna mixture on the double end of pastry and break an egg over it. Fold the unfilled pastry over the top to make an oblong shape, taking care not to press on it. Slip it into the hot, but not smoking, oil.
5 Fry the pastry for 2 minutes then turn and cook for another 1–2 minutes, until golden. Drain on kitchen paper. Repeat with the remaining ingredients.

CROSTINI DI FEGATO

Tuscan chicken liver toasts

A popular antipasto, crostini are pieces of toasted bread topped with a savoury spread – here a chicken liver paste.

INGREDIENTS

250g (8oz) fresh chicken livers
20g (¾oz) butter
15ml (1 tbsp) olive oil
1 small clove garlic, chopped
2 fresh sage leaves, finely chopped
salt and black pepper
squeeze of lemon
½ ciabatta loaf or other crusty Italian bread
1 tbsp very finely chopped fresh parsley

PREPARATION

1 Wash the chicken livers well, removing any greenish-tinged pieces, then chop them roughly.
2 Melt the butter with the oil in a frying pan over a high heat. Add the garlic and as soon as it starts to sizzle throw in the chicken livers, sage and seasoning. Fry for 2–3 minutes, stirring constantly, until the livers are brown all over.
3 Remove the pan from the heat, add the lemon juice and then mash the mixture with a fork to make a smooth paste.
4 Cut the ciabatta in half lengthways, and then cut into bite-sized squares. Toast the squares until golden on both sides. Spread the surface of each square with a little of the chicken liver mixture, sprinkle with parsley and serve.

FALAFEL

Chick-pea fritters

Illustrated on page 45.

INGREDIENTS

250g (8oz) dried chick-peas, soaked overnight
1 small red onion, chopped
2 cloves garlic, chopped
2 tsps ground coriander
2 tsps ground cumin
½ tsp cayenne pepper
1 tsp salt
½ tsp baking powder
3 tbsps chopped fresh parsley or coriander
sunflower or vegetable oil for deep-frying

PREPARATION

1 Drain the chick-peas and grind to a fine paste in a food processor. Add the onion and garlic and briefly process again.
2 Stir in the spices, salt, baking powder and parsley, and process again. It is important that the paste should be very fine.
3 Pour oil to a depth of 2.5cm (1in) into a pan and heat (it is ready when a cube of bread dropped in it turns golden). Form the paste into small patties and drop them into the oil. Fry for 3–4 minutes, until golden, drain on kitchen paper and serve hot.

BÖREKS

Turkish pastries

Illustrated on page 45.

INGREDIENTS

175g (6oz) feta cheese (drained weight)
2 tbsps finely chopped fresh chives or dill
2 tbsps finely chopped fresh parsley
½ tsp black pepper
90g (3oz) unsalted butter
8 sheets filo pastry

PREPARATION

1 Crumble the feta then mix with the herbs and pepper. Preheat the oven to 180°C/350°F/gas 4.
2 Melt the butter and skim off any scum.
3 Cut the filo pastry into 7cm (3in) strips. Take one strip and cover the rest with a damp tea towel.
4 Brush the strip with melted butter. Put a teaspoon of feta mixture on the bottom right-hand corner and fold up the pastry as shown on page 151.
5 Lay the pastries on a baking tray, brush with more butter and bake for 20 minutes.

DOLMATHES

Greek stuffed vine leaves

Illustrated on page 45 and opposite.

INGREDIENTS

250g (8oz) packet vine leaves in brine
(approximately 40 leaves)
150ml (¼ pint) olive oil
1 bunch spring onions, including green tops
600ml (1 pint) chicken stock (see page 155)
salt
175g (6oz) long-grain white rice, rinsed and drained
1 tsp ground cinnamon
90g (3oz) pine kernels
90g (3oz) raisins
juice of 1 lemon
1 fresh bay leaf
3 tbsps chopped fresh parsley
2 tbsps chopped fresh dill
1 tsp dried mint
2 lemons, cut into wedges, to serve

PREPARATION

1 Drain the vine leaves and place in a large bowl. Pour over just enough boiling water to cover them and soak for 20 minutes.
2 Heat 30ml (2 tbsps) of oil in a lidded saucepan. Finely chop the spring onions. Add to the pan and sauté for 5 minutes, until soft. Meanwhile bring the chicken stock to the boil, adding salt to taste.
3 Add the rice and cinnamon to the saucepan and stir well, making sure the grains of rice are coated in oil. Pour in the boiling stock and simmer, covered, for 10 minutes, until all the liquid has been absorbed and small holes start to appear in the surface of the rice.
4 Add the pine kernels and raisins to the rice, take the saucepan off the heat, cover with a dry tea towel, place the lid over the top and leave to stand for 15 minutes.
5 Drain the vine leaves and rinse well under cold running water. Line the base of a large heavy pan with leaves. Uncover the rice mixture and stir in half the lemon juice, the fresh herbs and dried mint.
6 To make each *dolma*, place a vine leaf on a board, stalk end towards you and fill and roll up, as shown opposite. Place each dolma join-side down in the pan, packing them tightly against each other.
7 Pour the remaining oil and lemon juice into the pan. Add just enough water to cover the dolmathes. Place a plate on top and weight it down. Set the pan over a gentle heat and cook for 1 hour.
8 Leave the dolmathes to cool in the liquid before lifting them out. Serve with wedges of lemon.

STUFFING A VINE LEAF

1 Place the vine leaf stalk end towards you. Put a teaspoon of rice just above the point where the stalk joins the leaf.

2 Using your finger and thumb, fold both sides of the vine leaf in towards the centre to hold in the stuffing mixture.

3 Firmly roll the leaf up from the stalk end to make a cylinder, keeping the sides tucked in and the stuffing intact.

VEGETABLE DISHES

One of the many reasons that the Mediterranean way of eating is good for you is the heavy emphasis on vegetables. They may be served as a first course, such as the classic Provençal Ratatouille, or may follow a meat or fish course. Many make excellent principle dishes, for example Parmigiana, a dish of aubergines baked with cheese, or Yemistes Piperies, Greek stuffed peppers. Although vegetables are rarely served alongside the main course in the Mediterranean, many of these dishes make superb accompaniments to plain grilled meat or fish.

SALATA JAZAR

Carrot salad

Larger late-season carrots work best for this vibrantly coloured purée pepped up with spices. As any Moroccan cook will tell you, the balance of spicing is highly individual — taste and alter the amounts to your own satisfaction.

INGREDIENTS

salt
500g (1lb) carrots
1 tsp sweet paprika
¼ tsp cayenne pepper
½ tsp ground cumin
¼ tsp ground cinnamon
½ tsp black pepper
½ tsp sugar
juice of ½ lemon
60ml (4 tbsps) olive oil
4 black olives

PREPARATION

1 Bring a large pan of heavily salted water to the boil. Peel the carrots and cook them whole for 15 minutes, or until tender, then drain.
2 Roughly chop the carrots and place them in a food processor with the spices, sugar and lemon juice. Purée until smooth, then slowly add the oil, beating, or keeping the processor on, to amalgamate it thoroughly.
3 When all the oil has been incorporated, taste the mixture to check the balance of flavours — you may need to adjust the seasoning, or add sugar or lemon juice, depending on the flavour of the carrots. Chill for 2 hours then serve garnished with black olives.

SALATA IL SHAMONDER

Beetroot salad

Provided beetroot is young and therefore small, it takes little time to cook from its raw state — and what a difference in taste from the familiar root pickled in sharp malt vinegar. This Syrian dish should convince those sceptical of the merits of beetroot that this vegetable is really worth the effort.

INGREDIENTS

750g (1½lb) raw young beetroot
1 small mild onion, finely chopped
1 clove garlic, finely chopped
2 tbsps chopped fresh parsley
juice of ½ lemon
90ml (3fl oz) olive oil
salt and black pepper

PREPARATION

1 Preheat the oven to 180°C/350°F/gas 4.
2 Wash the beetroot and bake in their skins for 1 hour, until wrinkled and soft. Alternatively, boil them in their skins — small roots will need about 30 minutes. As soon as they are cool enough to handle, peel and dice the beetroot and mix with the onion, garlic and parsley.
3 Beat together the lemon juice and oil and season well. Pour this dressing over the beetroot and leave to cool. Even though the salad is served cool, it is important to dress the beetroot while still warm.

VARIATIONS

• Dress the beetroot with a mixture of 250ml (8fl oz) of yogurt and 30ml (2 tbsps) of olive oil.
• Purée the salad in a food processor rather than leaving the beetroot in dice.

SALATA HORIATIKI

Peasant salad

There are many versions of this colourful Greek salad, but it must always include crumbly ewe's milk feta, sprinkled with oregano and Kalamata olives.

INGREDIENTS

2 small cucumbers
salt
4 large tomatoes, skinned
$\frac{1}{2}$ tsp sugar
1 cos lettuce heart
1 bunch spring onions
175g (6oz) feta cheese
2 tsps dried oregano (rigani)
2 tbsps capers, rinsed and drained
2 tbsps chopped fresh dill
16 Kalamata olives
juice of 1 lemon
125ml (4fl oz) extra-virgin olive oil

PREPARATION

1 Peel the cucumbers. Cut them in half lengthways and then across into fine half-moons. Place the cucumber slices in a colander and sprinkle with salt. Set aside for 20 minutes.
2 Cut the tomatoes in half and then slice into half-moons. Sprinkle the slices of tomato with salt and sugar and set them aside with the cucumber slices (this process helps to intensify the flavour).
3 Shred the lettuce. Finely chop the spring onions and lightly crumble the feta cheese. Rinse the cucumber slices and dry well on kitchen paper.
4 Choose a large round serving dish and make an outer circle of lettuce. Arrange the tomatoes in a ring inside and then make an inner ring of cucumber. Pile the feta cheese in the centre, then sprinkle it with oregano.
5 Scatter the capers, dill, spring onions and olives over the salad. Whisk the lemon juice and oil together and pour this dressing over the salad just before serving.

ENSALADA SEVILLANA

Sevillian salad

*This composite salad earns its Sevillian name through
the inclusion of ingredients for which the area is famous
– oranges and fat green manzanilla olives stuffed with
anchovies. Illustrated on page 82.*

INGREDIENTS

*1 lettuce, such as frisée or feuille de chêne
2 oranges, peeled
½ red onion
1 tbsp capers, rinsed and drained
90g (3oz) manzanilla olives stuffed with anchovies
1 clove garlic
yolk of 1 hard-boiled egg
30ml (2 tbsps) sherry vinegar
salt and black pepper
125ml (4fl oz) olive oil
1 tbsp chopped fresh tarragon*

PREPARATION

1 Shred the lettuce and wash and dry it well. Slice
the oranges across into thin rounds. Slice the onion
into fine half-moons.
2 Arrange the lettuce in a salad bowl, scatter with
the orange pieces and then sprinkle over the
capers, red onion and stuffed olives.
3 Crush the garlic using a pestle and mortar,
transfer it to a small bowl and mash it with the egg
yolk until you have a smooth paste.
4 Beat in the vinegar and a good grinding of salt
and pepper. Drip in the oil slowly, beating
continuously to amalgamate it thoroughly. Finish
the dressing with a scattering of fresh tarragon,
pour it over the salad and serve.

ANGINARES ME KOUKIA

Salad of artichokes with baby broad beans

*Artichokes and broad beans are in season at the same
time and Greek cooks have always combined them. Choose
baby broad beans and always remove the bitter outer skins.*

INGREDIENTS

*250g (8oz) baby broad beans in the pod
4 small globe artichokes
1 small bunch spring onions, including the green tops
90ml (3fl oz) olive oil
2 cloves garlic, finely chopped
juice of ½ lemon
salt and black pepper
3 tbsps chopped fresh parsley*

PREPARATION

1 Shell the beans and slip off the tough outer skins.
Prepare the artichokes (see page 150), cut the
hearts in half across or in quarters then put them
into water containing lemon juice or vinegar to
prevent discoloration.
2 Chop the spring onions into 1cm (½in) pieces.
In a large, wide pan gently heat the oil with the
spring onion and garlic. Cook for 5 minutes, then
add the artichokes, turning to coat them with oil.
3 Add the lemon juice, seasoning and 175ml
(6fl oz) of water. Bring to a slow simmer, cover the
pan and cook for 10 minutes.
4 Add the beans and most of the parsley, reserving
a little for a garnish. Cover and simmer for a
further 20 minutes, until almost all the liquid has
disappeared and the artichokes and beans are
tender. Serve just warm or cool, scattered with
the remaining parsley.

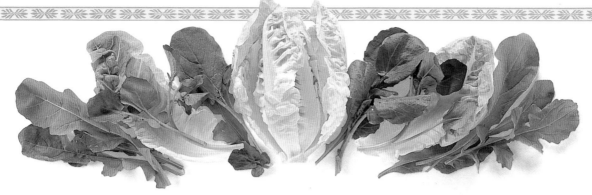

MESCLUN

Salad of young leaves

The people of the Mediterranean occasionally wander out in early summer to pick the bittersweet weeds of the fields and hillsides. The Provençal name for this selection of salad leaves comes from the Latin for "miscellany". Basically, anything goes provided it tastes good.

INGREDIENTS

125g (4oz) rocket
125g (4oz) young dandelion leaves, purslane or, failing that, watercress
2 small lettuce hearts or 1 large feuille de chêne heart
90ml (3fl oz) olive oil
juice of ½ lemon
salt and black pepper
4 tbsps chopped fresh chervil

PREPARATION

1 Wash all the leaves well and dry thoroughly, discarding any discoloured or wilted leaves.
2 Whisk together the olive oil and lemon juice with plenty of seasoning. Mix in the chervil. Dress the salad just before serving.

MANITARIA AFELIA

Mushrooms in red wine with coriander seeds

The Cypriots have a particular addiction to coriander seeds, the orange scent of which perfumes this dish of button mushrooms cooked in red wine. It can be served as a starter, part of a meze selection or with grilled meat.

INGREDIENTS

250g (8oz) small button mushrooms
60ml (4 tbsps) olive oil
125ml (4fl oz) red wine
salt and black pepper
1 tbsp coriander seeds, crushed

PREPARATION

1 Wipe the mushrooms clean, avoiding washing them if possible. Heat the olive oil over a medium heat and add the mushrooms. Fry, stirring continuously, for 5 minutes, until browned all over.
2 Pour the wine into the pan, allow to bubble hard for 1 minute then turn down to a simmer. Season, and cook uncovered for 8 minutes. Add the coriander seeds and cook for a further 2 minutes. Leave to cool slightly before serving.

CARCIOFI ALLA GIUDEA

Artichokes Jewish style

In many Mediterranean cities an individual style of cooking has developed in the Jewish community. Rome is no exception, and this dish of baby purple artichokes stewed in olive oil is now a favourite traditional dish throughout the town. Illustrated on page 83.

INGREDIENTS

12 very small and tender globe artichokes, stalks attached
2 lemons
8 cloves garlic, peeled
salt and black pepper
olive oil for stewing
2 tbsps finely chopped fresh parsley
1 tbsp finely chopped fresh mint

PREPARATION

1 Pull off the tough outer leaves of the artichokes. Trim the stalks, leaving 5cm (2in) intact. Cut in half lengthways and scoop out the choke (note that very small artichokes will have barely any choke). Place the artichokes in water mixed with lemon juice to prevent discoloration.
2 Put the garlic cloves in a heavy pan into which the drained artichokes fit snugly. Add plenty of seasoning and then pour in just enough olive oil to cover the artichokes. Cover the pan and place over a very low heat. Cook gently for 45 minutes – the artichokes should stew, not fry, in the oil.
3 Drain the artichokes, reserving the flavoured oil for later use, allow to cool, then sprinkle them with the chopped herbs. Serve with quarters of the remaining lemons.

CAPONATA

Sweet and sour aubergine, onion and celery salad

Tradition has that this dish was introduced to Sicily by the Moors, who needed to preserve their vegetables for sea voyages. They may have been forbidden to drink wine, but they made plentiful use of wine vinegar. The surviving dish is a delicate balance of Mediterranean vegetables in a sweet and sour sauce. It is sometimes served sprinkled with grated bitter chocolate.

INGREDIENTS

625g (1¼lb) aubergines
salt
1 onion
300ml (½ pint) olive oil
175g (6oz) celery, including leaves
500g (1lb) ripe plum tomatoes, skinned and chopped
125ml (4fl oz) red wine vinegar
1 tbsp white sugar
125g (4oz) cracked green olives
1 tbsp capers, rinsed and drained
black pepper
2 tbsps chopped fresh parsley

PREPARATION

1 Cut the aubergines into 2.5cm (1in) round slices, then cut each slice into quarters and salt and blot them (see page 150).

2 Peel the onion, cut in half and slice into fine half-moons. Heat 30ml (2 tbsps) of oil in a wide frying pan and cook the onion gently for 10 minutes, until translucent and soft.

3 Dice the celery and add to the onion along with the chopped celery leaves. Fry for a further 10 minutes, stirring regularly. Add the tomatoes and cook for a further 5 minutes.

4 Pour in the vinegar and stir in the sugar. Add the olives and capers. Simmer for 10 minutes until the tomatoes have broken down to form a thick sauce.

5 Pour the remaining oil into a frying pan to a depth of 2.5cm (1in) and warm over a medium heat. When the oil is very hot, add the rinsed and dried aubergine pieces. Fry for 5 minutes, stirring from time to time, until they are browned on all sides. Remove with a slotted spoon and drain on kitchen paper.

6 Stir the aubergine pieces into the tomato and celery mixture. Taste to check the balance of sweet and sour flavours – you may need to add a little more sugar. Season generously and then stir in the chopped parsley.

7 Leave the salad to stand for 24 hours, (preferably not in the refrigerator) to allow the flavours to mingle before serving.

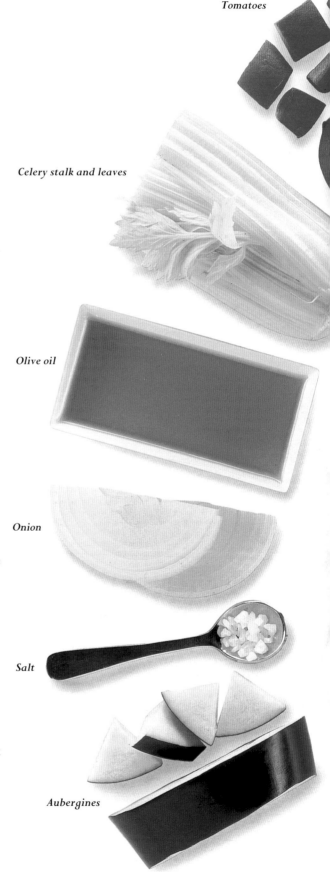

Tomatoes

Celery stalk and leaves

Olive oil

Onion

Salt

Aubergines

Red wine
vinegar

White
sugar

Cracked
green olives

Capers

Black
pepper

Parsley

PEPERONATA

Stewed peppers

Glossy with olive oil, red with tomato, this simple Italian dish brings out the best in sweet peppers. Prepare it several hours in advance to allow the flavours to develop.

INGREDIENTS

500g (1lb) mixed red and green peppers, cored and deseeded
100ml (3½ fl oz) olive oil
1 onion, finely chopped
2 cloves garlic, finely chopped
625g (1¼lb) plum tomatoes, skinned, deseeded and chopped
400g (13oz) can whole peeled tomatoes, chopped
salt and black pepper

PREPARATION

1 Cut the peppers into thin strips. Warm the oil in a heavy pan over a low heat and add the peppers, onion and garlic. Cover and stew for 30 minutes.
2 Add the fresh and canned tomatoes and seasoning. Leave barely simmering, uncovered, for 20 minutes. Allow to cool before serving.

ESPINACAS A LA CATALANA

Spinach Catalan style

Illustrated on page 38.

INGREDIENTS

3 tbsps raisins
2kg (4lb) fresh spinach
100ml (3½ fl oz) olive oil, plus oil for frying
1 clove garlic, finely chopped
3 tbsps pine kernels
salt and black pepper
2 slices white bread, crusts removed, cut into triangles

PREPARATION

1 Soak the raisins in hot water while preparing the spinach. Wash the spinach well and remove any tough stalks. Bring a large pan of salted water to the boil and cook the spinach for 3 minutes. Drain the spinach, plunge it into a large bowl of cold water and then drain again immediately.
2 Chop the spinach roughly. Put the oil in a heatproof pot and warm it over a very low heat. Add the garlic, pine kernels, drained raisins and spinach. Season well and cook for 20 minutes, stirring occasionally. Allow to stand for 15 minutes.
3 Meanwhile warm some oil over a medium heat and fry the bread until golden on both sides. Serve the spinach garnished with the bread triangles.

HABAS CON JAMON

Spanish broad beans with ham

Illustrated on page 39.

INGREDIENTS

1.5kg (3lb) baby broad beans in the pod
100ml (3½ fl oz) olive oil
125g (4oz) chunk Serrano ham or other cured ham, diced
salt and black pepper
2 tsps chopped fresh mint
juice of ½ lemon

PREPARATION

1 Shell the beans and slip off the tough outer skins, revealing the bright green halves of the bean.
2 Warm the oil in a heavy pan, preferably earthenware, over a medium heat. Add the beans and cook for 10 minutes.
3 Add the ham and seasoning (be careful with the salt as cured ham is already salty), then stir in the mint. Cook for a further 2–3 minutes before sprinkling with lemon juice.

CIPOLLINE IN AGRODOLCE

Sweet and sour baby onions

The Romans were especially fond of dishes that combined honey and vinegar for a sweet and sour flavour. Their heritage shows in this dish of caramelized onions. Serve hot with roast meat or cold with salami as antipasti.

INGREDIENTS

500g (1lb) baby onions no more than 3.5cm (1½in)
in diameter
30ml (2 tbsps) olive oil
2 cloves
1 bay leaf
60ml (2fl oz) red wine vinegar
1 tbsp sugar
salt and black pepper

PREPARATION

1 Bring a large pan of water to the boil. Add the onions in their skins, bring back to the boil and cook for 5 minutes. Remove from the heat, allow to cool, then skin them, taking care to leave them whole.
2 Warm the oil in a heavy pan over a medium to low heat. Add the cloves, bay leaf and onions. Cook for 20 minutes, turning the onions until browned.
3 Increase the heat and add the vinegar and sugar. Cook for 2 minutes until the pan juices acquire a syrupy consistency. Stir well to coat the onions, then season. Remove the cloves and bay leaf and serve.

RATATOUILLE

Vegetables stewed in olive oil

Ratatouille may be the definitive dish of Provence, but too often it becomes simply a vegetable stew. The key to ratatouille is that the vegetables, tomatoes apart, should hold their individual texture and flavours. They therefore need to be cooked separately before being put together in the pot.

INGREDIENTS

500g (1lb) aubergines
500g (1lb) large courgettes
salt
500g (1lb) mild onions
500g (1lb) red peppers, cored and deseeded
175ml (6fl oz) olive oil
6 cloves garlic, chopped
1kg (2lb) plum tomatoes, skinned, deseeded and chopped
3 sprigs fresh thyme
1 tbsp chopped fresh parsley
2 tbsps chopped fresh basil
4 coriander seeds
black pepper

PREPARATION

1 Cut the aubergines and courgettes across into slices 1cm (½in) thick. Place in separate colanders and salt and blot them (see page 150).
2 Peel the onions, cut in half and slice into fine half-moons. Cut the peppers into thin strips.
3 Heat half the oil in a large pan. When the oil is nearly spitting, add the rinsed and dried aubergine slices and fry for 3–4 minutes on each side, until soft and lightly browned. Remove and drain well on kitchen paper. Discard the oil.
4 Heat 60ml (4 tbsps) of oil and fry the courgette slices over a high heat for 3–4 minutes on each side, until lightly browned. Remove the courgettes and place them in a heavy pan with the cooked aubergine slices.
5 Fry the onions in the remaining oil over a gentle heat for 6–8 minutes, until just soft but not browned. Finally, fry the peppers for 5 minutes, until the skin is lightly wrinkled. Put all the vegetables together in the pan.
6 Heat the oil left in the pan and add the garlic. When the garlic starts to sizzle, add the chopped tomatoes, the herbs, coriander seeds, salt and pepper. Cook for 5 minutes, until the tomatoes are on the verge of breaking down.
7 Pour the tomato mixture over the vegetables in the pan and cook gently for 10 minutes.
8 Leave to cool, preferably not in the refrigerator. Ratatouille is best served the following day.

CHAKCHOUKA

Tunisian spicy peppers and tomatoes with eggs

This dish is similar to the Basque pipperrada – with the typical Tunisian addition of hot chillies. The eggs are left to cook whole among the vegetables. This dish should be served straight from the pan with plenty of bread to mop up the juices.

INGREDIENTS

1 large onion
3 green peppers, cored and deseeded
45ml (3 tbsps) olive oil
1 garlic clove, finely chopped
2 small fresh green chillies, deseeded and finely chopped
625g (1¼lb) plum tomatoes, skinned
salt and black pepper
4 large eggs

PREPARATION

1 Peel the onion, cut in half and slice into fine half-moons. Thinly slice the peppers. Warm the oil in a large, shallow heavy-based pan with a lid over a low heat. Add the onion. Stew very gently for 15 minutes, stirring occasionally, until the onions are soft. Do not allow them to brown.
2 Add the peppers, garlic and chillies to the onion. Cook for 20 minutes, until the peppers have softened and lost their bright green appearance.
3 Cut the tomatoes in half, or in quarters if they are large. Add them to the pan, cut-side down, and cook for a further 10 minutes, until the juices begin to run.
4 Season well, then make 4 wells in the mixture and carefully break a whole egg into each. Cover the pan and leave to cook until the eggs are just set, 6–7 minutes. Serve straight from the pan.

ENSALADA SEVILLANA
Sevillian salad
(page 76)

ESCALIVADA
Roasted peppers, aubergines
and onions
(page 88)

CARCIOFI ALLA GIUDEA
Artichokes Jewish style
(page 77)

BEIGNETS DE FLEURS DE COURGETTE

Provençal courgette flower fritters with fresh tomato sauce. Serves 6.

INGREDIENTS

24 small courgette flowers
150g (5oz) plain flour
1 tsp salt
2 large eggs, separated
15ml (1 tbsp) olive oil
350ml (12fl oz) full-cream milk
sunflower or vegetable oil for deep-frying

FRESH TOMATO SAUCE
750g (1½lb) plum tomatoes, skinned and deseeded
30ml (2 tbsps) olive oil
salt and black pepper
2 shallots, finely chopped
2 cloves garlic, finely chopped
1 tbsp torn fresh basil

PREPARATION

1 Carefully remove the stems and the long pistils inside the flowers.
2 Sieve the flour into a large bowl. Make a well in the centre and add the salt. Lightly beat the egg yolks and add them to the flour with the oil. Mix together with a wooden spoon, then beat in a little milk. Pour in the remaining milk in a steady stream while you continue to beat, until you have a smooth batter.
3 To make the sauce, put half the tomatoes in a sieve over a bowl. Press with the back of a wooden spoon to release the juice. Discard the flesh.
4 Beat the olive oil and seasoning into the tomato juice. Finely dice the remaining tomatoes and add to the juice with the shallots, garlic and basil. Place in the refrigerator until needed.
5 Take a large saucepan or deep-fryer, pour in oil to a depth of 10cm (4in) and heat. When the oil is almost ready (when a cube of bread dropped in it turns golden), whisk the egg whites until stiff and fold them into the batter.
6 Dip each flower in the batter and transfer to the hot oil. When the underside of the flower is golden (around 1 minute), turn it and fry for another minute. Never cook more than 3 flowers at a time.
7 Drain the fritters on kitchen paper. Serve immediately with the chilled tomato sauce.

VARIATION

• In Italy the flowers are fried in a light batter of 90g (3oz) plain flour to 300ml (½ pint) of iced water and served on their own or with grilled meat.

PATATAS BRAVAS

Spicy potatoes

Only the courageous should eat these potatoes, as their name suggests. There are many different versions of this dish in Spain, but they have one common characteristic – the potatoes are always spicy hot.

INGREDIENTS

750g (1½lb) waxy potatoes
60ml (4 tbsps) olive oil
salt and black pepper
2 tsps sweet paprika
½ tsp cayenne pepper
30ml (2 tbsps) red wine vinegar
2 tsps tomato purée

PREPARATION

1 Peel the potatoes and cut them into bite-sized chunks. Heat the oil in a heavy non-stick frying pan and add the potatoes. Fry for 3–4 minutes, turning frequently, until they are lightly coloured on all sides.
2 Season the potatoes, turn the heat to low and cover the pan. Leave the potatoes to cook for 20 minutes, shaking the pan halfway through.
3 Turn up the heat and sprinkle the potatoes with the paprika and cayenne. Stir well to coat.
4 Mix together the vinegar and tomato purée and pour into the pan – stand back as it will spit. Cook for 2 minutes, stirring constantly, until the potato pieces are well coated with a thick spicy sauce – there should be no liquid or oil left in the pan.

TORTILLA

Spanish potato omelette

Illustrated on page 39.

INGREDIENTS

4 large waxy potatoes
1 large Spanish onion
125ml (4fl oz) olive oil
5 large eggs
salt and black pepper

PREPARATION

1 Peel the potatoes and slice them very finely across (a mandolin or food processor makes this easy). Peel the onion, cut in half and slice into fine half-moons.
2 Warm three-quarters of the oil in a heavy frying pan over a low heat. Add the potatoes and onions, cover and leave to cook for 30 minutes, until they are soft but not coloured.
3 Remove the potatoes and onions from the pan with a slotted spoon and leave to cool for 10 minutes. Drain off any excess oil. Beat the eggs and season well. Add the potatoes and onions to the beaten eggs.
4 Return the pan to a low heat and add 15ml (1 tbsp) of oil. Add the egg, potato and onion mixture and cook until set in the centre, about 10 minutes.
5 Place an inverted plate over the pan and turn it upside down. Warm the remaining oil, slide the tortilla back in, uncooked-side down, and cook for 5 minutes. Serve warm or cold, cut into wedges.

CHAMPIÑONES AL AJILLO

Spanish mushrooms with garlic

Illustrated on page 38.

INGREDIENTS

500g (1lb) mushrooms
60ml (4 tbsps) olive oil
3 cloves garlic, finely chopped
salt and black pepper
juice of ½ lemon
2 tbsps chopped fresh parsley

PREPARATION

1 Clean the mushrooms – wipe wild ones with a damp cloth, rather than immerse them in water. Halve large mushrooms, but leave others whole.
2 Warm the oil in a frying pan over a medium heat. Add the garlic and fry for 1 minute then add the mushrooms. Fry for 5 minutes, stirring constantly, then season. Fry for a further 2 minutes then stir in the lemon juice and parsley.

FRITTATA DI ZUCCHINE

Courgette omelette

Some describe the frittata as the Italian version of the omelette, but apart from its use of eggs, the principles are quite different and the result is thick and juicy. My own summer favourite is made with courgettes, but sliced artichoke hearts also taste very good.

INGREDIENTS

1 large onion
30ml (2 tbsps) olive oil
500g (1lb) small courgettes
salt and black pepper
6 large eggs
60g (2oz) freshly grated Parmesan
30g (1oz) butter

PREPARATION

1 Peel the onion, cut in half and slice into fine half-moons. Heat the oil and fry the onion gently for 20 minutes, until very soft but not browned.
2 Slice the courgettes across at 5mm (¼in) intervals. Add the courgettes to the softened onion, season well and raise the heat to medium. Fry, stirring frequently, for 5 minutes.
3 Drain off any excess oil and discard. Leave the vegetables to cool for 10 minutes. Meanwhile beat the eggs with the Parmesan.
4 Stir the slightly cooled vegetable mixture into the eggs and cheese. Melt the butter in a non-stick frying pan approximately 30cm (12in) across over a low heat. When the butter begins to bubble, pour in the egg and vegetable mixture. Leave to cook over a low heat for 15 minutes.
5 Heat the grill to medium. When the frittata is almost set, place the pan under the grill for 2 minutes. Serve cold or hot.

YEMISTES PIPERIES

Stuffed peppers with tomato sauce

This Greek dish represents the principles of Mediterranean food, the main component being vegetables, made substantial with a rice and lamb filling. Variations using aubergines and tomatoes are also popular.

INGREDIENTS

8 small green peppers, tops sliced off, cored and deseeded
75ml (2½fl oz) olive oil
2 onions, finely chopped
3 cloves garlic, finely chopped
45ml (3 tbsps) red wine
1 tbsp honey
1 tbsp tomato purée
1.5kg (3lb) plum tomatoes, skinned and chopped
1 cinnamon stick
2 cloves
1 fresh bay leaf
salt and black pepper
350ml (12fl oz) chicken stock (see page 155)
250g (8oz) minced lamb
2 tsps ground cinnamon
2 tsps ground cumin
125g (4oz) long-grain rice, rinsed and drained

PREPARATION

1 Bring a pan of water to the boil and cook the peppers and tops for 5 minutes. Drain and set aside.
2 To make the sauce, heat half the oil and add half the onion and garlic. Stew gently for 10 minutes, until the onion is soft. Add the wine, honey and tomato purée and allow to bubble for 1 minute.
3 Add the tomatoes, cinnamon stick, cloves, bay leaf and seasoning. Leave to simmer, uncovered, for 30 minutes, until the sauce is thick.
4 Strain the sauce through a sieve and set aside. Heat the stock to boiling point.
5 To make the filling, warm the rest of the oil and add the remaining onion and garlic. Cook gently for 10 minutes, until the onion is soft. Turn up the heat and add the lamb, ground spices and seasoning. Fry for 2 minutes, stirring, to brown the meat.
6 Add the rice to the lamb mixture. Stir well, then pour over the boiling stock. Cook over a gentle heat for 15 minutes, until all the liquid has been absorbed and small holes begin to appear in the surface.
7 Preheat the oven to 180°C/350°F/gas 4. Stuff the peppers with the rice mixture and replace their tops. Pack them into a dish and pour over the sauce. Cover and bake for 1 hour. Allow to cool before serving – this dish is best made a day in advance.

PARMIGIANA

Aubergines baked with mozzarella and Parmesan

From Campania, the sun-baked southern tip of Italy, comes this basil-scented dish of aubergines smothered in tomato sauce and sandwiched between mozzarella and Parmesan. Classically, the aubergines are fried before being baked, but I prefer to grill them to reduce the amount of oil in the dish.

INGREDIENTS

750g (1½lb) aubergines
salt
75ml (2½fl oz) olive oil
1 onion, chopped
2 cloves garlic, finely sliced
1kg (2lb) plum tomatoes, skinned and deseeded or
625g (1¼lb) can whole peeled tomatoes
1 tsp tomato purée (omit if using canned tomatoes)
1 tsp chopped fresh oregano
salt and black pepper
200g (7oz) mozzarella (drained weight)
125g (4oz) freshly grated Parmesan
good handful of basil leaves

PREPARATION

1 Cut the aubergines lengthways into 1cm (½in) wide strips and salt and blot them (see page 150).
2 Meanwhile, make the tomato sauce. Heat 45ml (3 tbsps) of oil in a heavy pan over a low heat. Add the onion and garlic. Sweat gently for 20 minutes.
3 Turn up the heat and add the tomatoes and tomato purée, if using. Add the oregano and seasoning and allow to bubble for 5 minutes, stirring regularly to break down the tomatoes.
4 Preheat the grill to maximum. Place the rinsed and dried aubergines on a metal baking sheet, dribble over a little oil and grill for 5 minutes. Turn the aubergines, dribble with the remaining oil and grill for a further 5 minutes. Slice the mozzarella.
5 Preheat the oven to 180°C/350°F/gas 4. Take a deep round earthenware dish and cover the base with a layer of tomato sauce. Lay some aubergine strips on top, followed by three-quarters of the mozzarella and half the Parmesan. Season well.
6 Add the basil leaves. Top with the remaining aubergines and mozzarella, pour over the rest of the tomato sauce and sprinkle over the remainder of the Parmesan. Bake in the oven for 30 minutes.

ESCALIVADA
Roasted peppers, aubergines and onions

The three vegetables that comprise Escalivada are traditionally roasted over charcoal, but today most Catalans cook them in the oven. Whatever method is used, the sweetness of the vegetables is brought to the fore. For a more substantial dish, finish with a scattering of flakes of cooked tuna or salt cod. *Illustrated on page 83.*

INGREDIENTS
750g (1½lb) red peppers
750g (1½lb) aubergines
500g (1lb) onions (in their skins)
salt
60ml (4 tbsps) extra-virgin olive oil
1 clove garlic, finely chopped

PREPARATION
1 Preheat the oven to 180°C/350°F/gas 4. Place the peppers, aubergines and onions on a baking tray and bake for 1 hour, or until tender.
2 Remove the tray from the oven and cover the vegetables with a tea towel. Leave for 10 minutes.
3 Remove the blistered skin of the peppers (see page 150) and scrape out the seeds. Cut the flesh into strips. Remove the skin of the aubergines and cut the flesh lengthways into strips. Peel the onions and roughly chop the flesh.
4 Arrange the roasted vegetables in a serving dish. Sprinkle liberally with salt and oil, scatter over the chopped garlic. Leave to cool before serving.

HUEVOS REVUELTOS CON ESPARRAGOS
Scrambled eggs with asparagus

I cannot imagine a more indulgent supper than this simple Spanish dish. It is traditionally made with wild asparagus: look for the very thin sprues.

INGREDIENTS
500g (1lb) asparagus
5 large eggs
good pinch each of sweet paprika and ground cumin
salt and black pepper
30ml (2 tbsps) olive oil
30g (1oz) butter

PREPARATION
1 Trim the woody ends from the asparagus, removing the tough fibrous outer layer with a potato peeler if the stalks are large. Cut the asparagus into 2.5cm (1in) lengths, setting aside the tips.
2 Bring a pan of salted water to the boil and add the asparagus, excluding the tips. Boil thin sprues for 2 minutes, thicker asparagus for 4 minutes. Add the tips and boil for a further 2 minutes. Drain carefully – the asparagus should be just tender.
3 Beat the eggs with the spices and seasoning.
4 Warm the olive oil with the butter in a large heavy pan over a moderate heat. When the butter has melted and the oil is sizzling, add the eggs. Stir for 1 minute with a wooden spoon, then add the asparagus. Cook for a further minute, until the eggs are just set, and serve at once.

YOĞURTLU PATLICAN
Fried aubergines with yogurt

Thick creamy yogurt is often used in Turkey to dress raw and cooked vegetables, here fried aubergines. For a lighter dish, brush the aubergines with oil and grill them until golden brown before topping with the spicy yogurt.

INGREDIENTS
900g (1¾lb) large aubergines
salt
150ml (¼ pint) olive oil
300ml (½ pint) strained natural yogurt
2 cloves garlic, peeled and crushed
1 tsp caraway seeds
salt and black pepper
½ tsp sweet paprika
1 tbsp chopped fresh dill

PREPARATION
1 Cut the aubergines across into 1cm (½in) slices. Salt and blot them (see page 150).
2 Heat the oil in a frying pan over a medium-high heat. When the oil is nearly ready (when a cube of bread dropped in it turns golden), add a few rinsed and dried aubergine slices. Fry for 1 minute on each side until golden, remove with a slotted spoon and drain on kitchen paper.
3 Continue the process until all the aubergine slices are cooked. Do not add too many slices to the frying pan at once and make sure that the oil is very hot or the aubergines will absorb too much oil.
4 Mix together the yogurt, garlic, caraway seeds and seasoning. Lay the fried aubergine slices on a plate and pour over the spiced yogurt. Sprinkle with the paprika and dill. The aubergines can be served warm or cold, but should be dressed with the yogurt while still hot.

TUMBET

Baked vegetables

Rich in olive oil, this Majorcan dish makes a substantial main course and is often served on the island with slices of sausage and cured pork. In some versions the potatoes are replaced by dried breadcrumbs.

INGREDIENTS

500g (1lb) aubergines
salt
250ml (8fl oz) olive oil
500g (1lb) small waxy potatoes, peeled and sliced
500g (1lb) green peppers, cored, deseeded and cut into strips
5 cloves garlic
1.25kg (2½lb) plum tomatoes, skinned and chopped
black pepper
pinch of sugar, optional

PREPARATION

1 Slice the aubergines thinly across. Salt and blot them (see page 150).
2 Heat the oil in a large heavy frying pan. When the oil is just beginning to sizzle, add the potato slices. Fry for 5 minutes, turning them regularly, until lightly browned. Remove with a slotted spoon and drain on kitchen paper.
3 Add the peppers to the oil and fry for 2–3 minutes, until just coloured. Remove with a slotted spoon and drain on kitchen paper.
4 Fry the rinsed and drained aubergines in two batches in the oil, until golden on both sides. Remove and drain on kitchen paper.
5 Preheat the oven to 190°C/375°F/gas 5. Drain off all but 2 tablespoons of the oil and return the pan to the heat. Add the garlic and, as soon as it starts to sizzle, add the tomatoes. Keep the heat high and cook the tomatoes for 5 minutes, stirring all the time, until they break down.
6 Push the resulting tomato sauce through a fine sieve and season to taste, adding a pinch of sugar if the tomatoes are not very flavourful.
7 Arrange the fried vegetables in layers in an earthenware lidded casserole, starting with potatoes and ending with aubergines, and seasoning as you go.
8 Pour over the tomato sauce, cover the dish and place in the preheated oven for 30 minutes. Allow to stand for 20 minutes before serving.

SPANAKOPITA

Spinach pie

This spiced spinach pie with an orange-flavoured crust is a favourite Greek picnic dish. If you don't have time to make your own pastry, use layers of filo, brushed with olive oil.

INGREDIENTS

PASTRY
300g (10oz) plain flour
1 tsp salt
30ml (2 tbsps) olive oil
60–75ml (4–5 tbsps) freshly squeezed orange juice
1 small egg, separated
SPINACH FILLING
750g (1½lb) spinach, washed and trimmed
60ml (4 tbsps) olive oil
1 onion, finely chopped
salt and black pepper
1 tsp ground cumin
juice of 1 lemon
3 tbsps chopped fresh dill
2 tbsps sesame seeds

PREPARATION

1 To make the pastry, sieve the flour and salt into a bowl. Make a well in the centre and add the olive oil and orange juice. Lightly whip the egg white, add to the flour and work the mixture together.
2 With floured hands, knead the pastry for 5 minutes, until it loses its stickiness and becomes pliable. Wrap it in clingfilm and chill for 1 hour.
3 Put the spinach in a pan with 30ml (2 tbsps) of water, cover and cook gently until wilted. Drain and, when cool enough to handle, squeeze dry.
4 Heat 30ml (2 tbsps) of oil over a low heat and add the onion. Cook for 10 minutes until soft. Add the spinach, seasoning, cumin, lemon juice and dill. Cook gently for a further 5 minutes, until any liquid has evaporated.
5 Preheat the oven to 180°C/350°F/gas 4. Oil a 23cm (9in) tart tin. Take two-thirds of the pastry and put the remainder back in the refrigerator. Dip your hands in a bowl of iced water. Flour a surface and roll out the pastry to fit the tart tin. Trim the edges and then fill the pie with the spinach mixture.
6 Roll out the remaining pastry to form a crust, sealing the edges with iced water. Brush the crust with the remainder of the oil and place in the oven.
7 After 30 minutes, turn the heat down to 150°C/300°F/gas 2. Brush with beaten egg yolk and sprinkle over the sesame seeds. Return to the oven and bake for another 30 minutes, until the sesame seeds are toasted. Serve warm or cold.

FISH DISHES

The Mediterranean region is defined by its sea, and it is the fruits of that water that most characterize Mediterranean cooking. A visit to the local fish market will reveal a bewildering array of colours and shapes: tiny glinting silver fish for the frying pan, the vermilion shine of red mullet, thick steaks of tuna and swordfish, piles of tiny squid no bigger than a thumbnail. Then there are the shellfish stalls, stacked high with mussels and clams, prawns, crabs and lobsters of all varieties and sizes. The choice is endless and all find their way into the cooking pot.

ALMEJAS A LA MARINERA

Clams with white wine and garlic sauce

No tapas bar is complete without shellfish. There may be a few stuffed mussels, a shellfish salad or this dish of clams cooked in a white wine and garlic sauce. The little clam shells serve as receptacles with which to scoop up the sauce.

INGREDIENTS

1kg (2lb) live clams
3fl oz (90ml) olive oil
1 small white onion, finely chopped
4 cloves garlic, finely chopped
1 small dried red chilli, finely chopped
1 tbsp plain flour
250ml (8fl oz) medium-dry white wine
2 tsps sweet paprika
salt and black pepper
1 bay leaf
2 tbsps finely chopped fresh parsley

PREPARATION

1 Clean the clams (see page 153).
2 Heat the oil in an earthenware dish or, failing that, a heavy pan over a gentle heat. Add the onion, garlic and chilli and sauté for 15 minutes, stirring regularly, until the onion is tinged with yellow.
3 Turn up the heat to medium and add the clams. Cook until all the clams open (3–4 minutes), discarding any that have not opened, then stir in the flour, followed by the wine.
4 Add the paprika, salt and pepper to taste (be careful with the salt as the liquid the clams release is salty), the bay leaf and parsley. Simmer for 5 minutes, stirring regularly, until the sauce has thickened. Check the seasoning and serve.

ESQUEIXADA

Salt cod salad

Salt cod, traditionally served on Fridays and during Lent, remains very popular in the west of the Mediterranean region. It needs long soaking and is often poached. In this Catalan salad, however, the salt cod is not cooked but simply marinated and shredded.

INGREDIENTS

500g (1lb) salt cod
1 green pepper, peeled, cored and deseeded
1 red pepper, peeled, cored and deseeded
1 small mild onion
1 small clove garlic
2 large tomatoes, skinned, deseeded and chopped
125ml (4fl oz) olive oil
30ml (2 tbsps) red wine vinegar
black pepper
60g (2oz) small black olives

PREPARATION

1 Soak the salt cod for 24 hours, changing the water several times. Remove the skin and bone and shred the flesh finely with your fingers. Do not be tempted to use a knife.
2 Finely dice the flesh of the peppers. Peel the onion and cut into very thin rings.
3 Cut the garlic clove in half and rub the cut side around an earthenware serving dish. Mix together the peppers, onion, tomatoes and the shredded salt cod and place in the dish.
4 Beat together the oil and vinegar to form an emulsion, add a generous grinding of pepper and pour this dressing over the salad. Leave to marinate for at least 4 hours. Garnish the salad with olives before serving.

SALPICON DE MARISCOS

Spanish shellfish salad

INGREDIENTS

750g (1½lb) live mussels and clams
375g (12oz) cooked large prawns
90ml (3fl oz) olive oil
30ml (2 tbsps) sherry vinegar
2 tbsps capers, rinsed and drained
4 small pickled gherkins, finely chopped
1 tbsp chopped bottled red pimiento pepper
½ mild white onion, chopped
2 tbsps chopped fresh parsley
salt and black pepper

PREPARATION

1 Clean the mussels and clams (see page 153). Steam them open in 4 tablespoons of water. As soon as they are cool enough to handle, remove most of them from their shells, reserving a few in their shells as a garnish, if desired. Discard any that have not opened. Peel the cooked prawns.

2 Beat together the oil and vinegar until emulsified. Mix with the remaining ingredients. Pour this marinade over the prawns and shelled mussels and clams, being careful to coat all the shellfish thoroughly.

3 Chill for at least 4 hours, preferably overnight, to allow the flavours to mingle before serving.

SAMAK MESHWI BI TAHINI

Grilled fish with sesame sauce

*This sesame seed sauce is especially popular in
Syria and Lebanon. Sharp with lemon juice, it is often
served with cold fish steaks but is equally good with
a herb-stuffed whole fish, grilled or, better still,
cooked over charcoal.*

INGREDIENTS

*1 fish, such as grey mullet, sea bass, sea bream,
weighing approximately 1.25kg (2½lb), scaled
and gutted (see page 152)
45ml (3 tbsps) olive oil
salt
6 tbsps chopped fresh parsley
3 tbsps chopped fresh coriander
4 cloves garlic
250ml (8fl oz) tahini paste
juice of 4 lemons*

PREPARATION

1 Wash the fish well and make 4 deep slashes
across the flesh on either side. Rub in plenty of
olive oil and salt and leave to stand for 1 hour.
2 Mix together half the parsley and all the
coriander. Finely dice two of the garlic cloves and
mix with the herbs. Stuff this mixture into the
cavity of the fish.
3 To make the tahini sauce, beat 60ml (4 tbsps) of
water into the tahini paste – surprisingly, this will
thicken it. Add the lemon juice to thin it.
4 Using a pestle and mortar, crush the remaining
garlic to a paste with ½ teaspoon of salt, then add
the remaining parsley and crush again. Mix this
paste into the tahini and lemon mixture.
5 Preheat the grill to hot and grill the fish for
8 minutes on either side, until you can see clearly
through to the bone and the skin is nicely blackened.
Serve the fish either hot or cold with the sauce.

KILIÇ SISTE TARATOR

Turkish swordfish kebabs with walnut sauce

Illustrated on page 51.

INGREDIENTS

*750g (1½lb) swordfish, cut into steaks
at least 2.5cm (1in) thick
juice of 1 lemon
60ml (4 tbsps) olive oil
1 tsp sweet paprika
salt and black pepper
16 fresh bay leaves*
TARATOR SAUCE
*100g (3½oz) shelled walnuts
3 cloves garlic
½ tsp sea salt
2 slices white country-style bread, crusts removed
150ml (¼ pint) olive oil
juice of 1 lemon*

PREPARATION

1 Cut the swordfish into 2.5cm (1in) cubes and
place in an earthenware dish.
2 Beat together the lemon juice and olive oil so
that they emulsify, then add the paprika and
seasoning. Pour this marinade over the swordfish,
turning the cubes to coat them thoroughly. Leave
to marinate in a cool place or in the refrigerator
for a minimum of 4 hours (preferably overnight).
3 Pour boiling water over the bay leaves. Leave for
1 hour and then drain.
4 Meanwhile, make the walnut sauce. Grind
together the walnuts, garlic and salt until you have
a coarse paste. You can use a pestle and mortar and
this traditional method achieves the best result, but
a food processor is a satisfactory alternative.
5 Briefly soak the bread in water then squeeze it
dry. Using the back of a wooden spoon, combine
the walnut paste with the soaked bread.
6 Whisk together the oil and lemon juice until
they emulsify, then very gradually beat this
emulsification into the walnut mixture, until you
have a smooth sauce.
7 When you are ready to cook the kebabs, preheat
the grill to medium or make sure the charcoals are
just glowing. Thread 4 cubes of fish onto each
kebab stick, interspersing them with bay leaves.
8 Cook the kebabs for 15 minutes, turning them
halfway through and basting the fish frequently
with the marinade. Serve straight from the grill
accompanied by a bowl of walnut sauce.

CALAMARES A LA PLANCHA
Grilled squid

Cooking a la plancha, *or on the hot plate, is a favourite way of preparing food in Spain. Chipirones, squid the size of a thumbnail, are special delicacies, but the method also works well with slightly larger squid, provided they have been marinated.*

INGREDIENTS

500g (1lb) very small fresh squid
45ml (3 tbsps) olive oil
45ml (3 tbsps) dry white wine
2 cloves garlic, finely chopped
2 tbsps finely chopped fresh parsley
1 tsp sweet paprika
salt and black pepper
juice of ½ lemon

PREPARATION

1 Prepare the squid (see page 153). Using a sharp knife cut halfway up one side of each body sac. Mix together the oil and the wine and pour over the cleaned squid. Leave to stand for at least 2 hours.
2 Heat an oiled cast-iron griddle or, alternatively, place a metal baking tray beneath a hot grill. Remove the squid from the marinade and pat dry with kitchen paper. Mix the garlic with the parsley.
3 When the griddle or baking tray is very hot, throw on the squid. Cook for 1 minute, until the tentacles curl up and the body sacs turn inside out to form little conical hat shapes. Sprinkle on the garlic and parsley mixture, the paprika and plenty of seasoning. Cook for a further 30 seconds. Finish with the lemon juice and serve at once.

LOUP DE MER GRILLE AU FENOUIL
Sea bass grilled with fennel

The sea bass, the king of fish, is traditionally barbecued over wild fennel branches in Provence. For days when this is hardly feasible, try grilling the fish and serving it with fennel stewed in olive oil.

INGREDIENTS

750g (1½lb) sea bass, scaled and gutted (see page 152)
4 small fennel bulbs
2 lemons, sliced
90ml (3fl oz) olive oil
salt and black pepper
2 garlic cloves, peeled

PREPARATION

1 With a sharp knife make 3 deep slashes across each side of the sea bass. Remove the stalks and feathery fronds of the fennel bulbs and stuff them into the cavity of the fish. Slip in 2 slices of lemon and dribble 30ml (2 tbsps) of oil over the fish, then season generously.
2 Cut the fennel bulbs in quarters. Warm the remaining oil with the whole cloves of garlic in a heavy frying pan over a medium-low heat. Add the quartered fennel bulbs and season to taste. Cook gently in the oil, turning frequently, for 45 minutes, until the fennel is browned and soft all the way through. Remove the garlic cloves and discard.
3 Preheat the grill to hot and grill the fish for 12 minutes on either side, until cooked through to the bone. Serve surrounded by stewed fennel and garnished with the remaining lemon slices.

OKTAPOTHI STI SKARA
Grilled octopus

Rows of octopuses hanging up to dry in the hot sun are a familiar sight all over Greece. After a few days of this treatment, they are grilled on the barbecue and served with a glass of ouzo.

INGREDIENTS

1 octopus weighing approximately 1kg (2lb)
500ml (16fl oz) dry white wine
2 sprigs fresh rosemary
4 sprigs fresh oregano
8 peppercorns
200ml (7fl oz) olive oil
juice of 2 lemons, plus 2 lemons, quartered, to serve
salt

PREPARATION

1 Remove the eyes and head of the octopus, if necessary, leaving the body and tentacles whole.
2 Place the octopus in a pan and pour over the wine, adding water if necessary to cover it. Bring slowly to the boil and simmer for 1¼ hours, until the octopus is tender. Remove the octopus and cut the flesh into 2.5cm (1in) pieces.
3 Place the octopus pieces in an earthenware bowl and cover with the sprigs of herbs and the peppercorns. Whisk together the olive oil and lemon juice and pour over the octopus. Leave to marinate overnight.
4 Grill the octopus, preferably over charcoal, for 4–5 minutes, brushing it with the marinade during cooking. Sprinkle liberally with salt and serve with quarters of lemon.

SARDALYA SARMASI
Stuffed sardines in vine leaves
(page 102)

**COQUILLES ST. JACQUES
A LA PROVENÇALE**
*Scallops with garlic
and Cognac*
(page 97)

BOUILLABAISSE
Marseillais fish stew
(page 97)

PESCE ALLA GRIGLIA SALSA VERDE

Italian grilled fish with green sauce

Illustrated on page 51.

INGREDIENTS

1kg (2lb) small red mullet
60g (2oz) finely chopped fresh parsley
50g (1¾oz) anchovies in olive oil, drained and finely chopped
2 tbsps capers, rinsed, drained and finely chopped
2 cloves garlic, finely chopped
juice of 1 lemon
175ml (6fl oz) olive oil, plus oil to grease
black pepper

PREPARATION

1 Clean, scale and gut the mullet (see page 152). Lay them on an oiled baking sheet or barbecue rack. Preheat the grill to maximum or make sure the charcoals are glowing.
2 Make the salsa verde by mixing the parsley, anchovy, capers, garlic, lemon juice, oil and pepper.
3 Grill the fish for 5–10 minutes, according to their size and thickness, turning them halfway through cooking. Serve them with the salsa verde.

FRITTO MISTO DI MARE

Deep-fried fish

This dish, prepared with the catch of the day, was my favourite Sunday lunch when I was a child in Italy. I loved the surprise of finding the different types of fish when I bit into the crispy, olive oil-flavoured coating. You can use larger fish cut into pieces or other shellfish.

INGREDIENTS

250g (½lb) small squid, prepared (see page 153)
olive oil for deep-frying
250g (½lb) raw prawns, peeled
250g (½lb) very small fish, such as whitebait
salt and black pepper
flour, to coat the fish
2 lemons, quartered

PREPARATION

1 Cut the squid bodies into rings, leaving the tentacles whole. Heat plenty of olive oil in a deep-fryer. Season the squid, prawns and fish well, then roll in the flour, shaking off any excess.
2 When the oil is hot enough to crisp a piece of bread, add the fish in batches and fry until golden. Drain on kitchen paper. Serve with lemon quarters.

BOURRIDE

Provençal fish stew

A rich creamy broth made with white fish steaks and thickened with aïoli, a garlicky mayonnaise. Serves 6–8.

INGREDIENTS

1kg (2lb) fish trimmings
2 carrots, peeled
2 sticks celery, chopped
stalk of 1 fennel bulb
1 onion, peeled
125ml (4fl oz) dry vermouth
2 sprigs parsley
piece of orange zest
salt and black pepper
6 fat cloves garlic, peeled
½ tsp salt
6 large egg yolks, at room temperature
300ml (½ pint) olive oil
1.5kg (3lb) mixed white fish steaks, such as monkfish, John Dory, sea bass, sea bream, whiting, cod, turbot
6 slices country-style bread

PREPARATION

1 Prepare the stock. Simmer together the fish trimmings, 2 litres (3½ pints) of water, carrots, celery, fennel, onion, vermouth, parsley, orange zest and seasoning for 30 minutes, then strain.
2 Meanwhile, make the aïoli. Make sure all the ingredients are at room temperature. Using a pestle and mortar, pound the garlic and salt until you have a paste. Add 2 egg yolks and pound again.
3 Next, add just a drop of oil and pound until amalgamated. Continue adding the oil drop by drop until you have a thick emulsion – do not rush or it will curdle. When you have a thick mixture, add the remaining oil in a thin stream, pounding steadily.
4 Place the fish in a pot over a medium heat. Pour over just enough stock to cover them. Bring to a slow simmer. Cook for 10–15 minutes, or until the fish starts to flake.
5 Remove the fish from the stock and transfer to a low oven to keep warm. Measure out 1.25 litres (2 pints) of stock and leave to cool for 5 minutes.
6 Take half the aïoli and beat the remaining egg yolks into it. Add a ladle of stock to the aïoli and egg mixture, beat well, then pour in the remaining stock.
7 Pour this mixture into a double boiler and warm gently, beating all the time, until it has a creamy consistency. Do not allow it to boil and curdle.
8 Toast the bread and lay a slice in each soup bowl. Arrange the fish on a serving dish, garnished with the remaining aïoli. Pour the creamy broth over the bread and serve.

BOUILLABAISSE

Marseillais fish stew

The people of Marseilles will tell you that it is impossible to make an authentic bouillabaisse outside their city, for you will never find the little rock fish sold in their markets specifically for this classic dish. Do at least try to use a wide variety of fish. Serves 8.
Illustrated on page 95.

INGREDIENTS

2.5kg (5lb) fish (including some rock fish, such as rascasse or scorpion fish, weever fish, star gazer, gurnard, and at least 6 of the following: wrasse, conger eel, red mullet, monkfish, John Dory, sea bream, whiting
3 onions
3 leeks
2 black peppercorns
500ml (16fl oz) dry white wine
½ tsp saffron
1 slightly stale baguette
250ml (8fl oz) olive oil
6 cloves garlic, peeled
750g (1½lb) plum tomatoes, skinned
2 cloves
bouquet garni made up of 1 fresh bay leaf, 1 sprig fresh thyme, 2 fennel fronds and a piece of dried orange zest
salt and black pepper
ROUILLE
6 cloves garlic, peeled
½ tsp salt
2–3 small dried red chillies, chopped
2 slices day-old bread, crusts removed
150ml (5fl oz) olive oil

PREPARATION

1 Remove the heads of the fish and place them in a pan. Add 1 whole onion, a leek, the peppercorns, wine and 2.5 litres (4 pints) of water. Simmer for 20 minutes and then strain.
2 Cut the bodies of the larger fish into slices, leaving the smaller rock fish whole. Toast the saffron strands briefly and grind to a powder.
3 To make the rouille, crush the garlic, salt and chillies together to make a paste. Briefly soak the bread in a little water, squeeze dry and add to the paste. Pound until amalgamated. Gradually add the oil, drop by drop, so that it is amalgamated (this stage can be done using a food processor, but a pestle and mortar gives the best result).
4 Cut the baguette into 3.5cm (1½in) slices and bake in the oven until brown and dry.
5 Finely chop the remaining onions, leeks and 5 of the garlic cloves. Heat 60ml (4 tbsps) of oil in a large pan over a low heat and add the onion, leeks

and garlic. Stew slowly for 5 minutes – the vegetables should soften but not brown.
6 Add the tomatoes and cook slowly for a further 5 minutes, until they have broken down.
7 Meanwhile, bring the strained stock to the boil and add the remaining oil and crushed saffron. Stir in the cloves, bouquet garni and plenty of seasoning. Boil hard for 5 minutes to amalgamate the liquid and oil.
8 Add the fish: first firmer fish steaks, such as conger eel and monkfish, then the fish slices. After 7–8 minutes add the small fish. Cook for a further 5 minutes at a fast boil.
9 Check the soup's seasoning and discard the bouquet garni. Remove the fish from the soup and place on a warmed platter, then pour the broth into a large tureen (alternatively you can serve the fish and broth together in individual soup bowls). Serve the toasted bread with rouille separately, for each diner to help themselves.

COQUILLES ST. JACQUES A LA PROVENÇALE

Scallops with garlic and Cognac

The key to cooking scallops is to do so very quickly so that they remain juicy and tender – as in this simple yet luxurious recipe from the South of France, which is a favourite of mine. If you buy scallops on the shell, keep the shells to serve them in.
Illustrated on page 94.

INGREDIENTS

16 large scallops, preferably with corals
salt and black pepper
2 tbsps plain flour
60ml (4 tbsps) olive oil
4 cloves garlic, very finely chopped
30ml (2 tbsps) Cognac
4 tbsps chopped fresh parsley

PREPARATION

1 Clean the scallops, if necessary (see page 153). Slice the white part of the scallops in half, leaving the corals whole. Season all the pieces well, then sprinkle them with a little flour.
2 Heat the oil in a heavy pan. Scatter in the garlic and when it begins to sizzle put in the white parts of the scallops. Cook for no more than 1 minute.
3 Add the corals and cook for a further minute, turning the white parts. Stand back, pour in the Cognac, and as soon as it sizzles take the pan off the heat and sprinkle over the parsley. Serve in the scallop shells or on slices of toast.

ROMESCO DE PEIX

Seafood stew with romesco pepper sauce

*This classic dish from Tarragona, the Roman
city on the coast south of Barcelona, takes its name from
the romesco, or nyora, chilli pepper traditionally used.
The sauce in which the fish is cooked is very garlicky,
thick with nuts and wonderfully aromatic.*

INGREDIENTS

*1 large mild dried red chilli, preferably romesco
60g (2oz) blanched hazelnuts
60g (2oz) blanched almonds
750g (1½lb) mixed white fish steaks, such as monkfish,
sea bass, swordfish or sea bream
salt and black pepper
1 tbsp plain flour, plus flour for dusting
90ml (3fl oz) olive oil
2 small dried red chillies
1 bulb garlic
1 slice white bread, crusts removed
2 tbsps chopped fresh parsley
175ml (6fl oz) dry white wine
475ml (15½fl oz) fish stock (see page 155)
500g (1lb) live clams or live mussels*

PREPARATION

1 Soak the large chilli in warm water for 1 hour.
Toast the nuts in a dry frying pan.
2 Cut the fish into 5–7cm (2–3in) pieces, season
well and dust lightly with flour. Heat 60ml (4 tbsps)
of oil in a large pan and fry the fish for 5 minutes,
turning halfway through, until golden, then set aside.
3 Drain the romesco pepper and chop finely; chop
the small chillies. Peel all the garlic cloves and set
aside half. Warm the oil in which the fish was fried
and add the chopped chillies and half the garlic.
Fry for 2 minutes.
4 Warm 15ml (1 tbsp) of oil in a separate frying
pan and fry the slice of bread until golden.
5 In a food processor, process the hazelnuts and
almonds, both types of chilli, the cooked and raw
garlic, fried bread, parsley and 60ml (4 tbsps) of
wine to a paste.
6 Heat the remaining oil in the large pan. Add the
paste and 1 tablespoon of flour. Cook gently for
2 minutes, stirring to amalgamate the flour, then
slowly pour in the remaining wine. Finally, add the
fish stock and seasoning. Simmer for 5 minutes,
stirring all the time, until the sauce thickens.
7 Meanwhile, clean the clams (see page 153).
8 Place the fish steaks and the shellfish in the large
pan, coating them with sauce. Allow to simmer,
uncovered, for 10 minutes, until the fish is tender
and the shellfish have opened. Serve immediately.

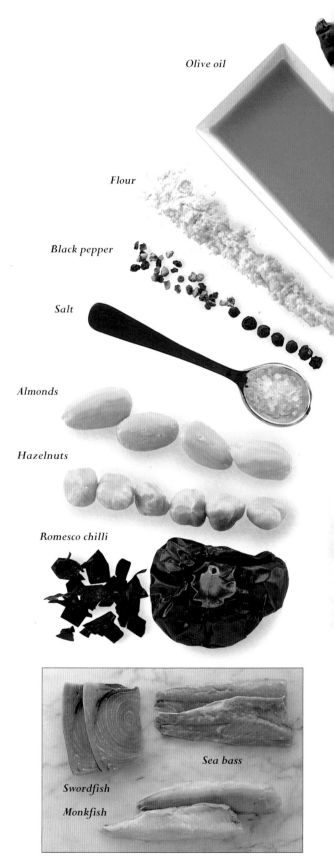

Olive oil

Flour

Black pepper

Salt

Almonds

Hazelnuts

Romesco chilli

Swordfish

Sea bass

Monkfish

Small dried
chillies

Garlic

White
bread

Parsley

White wine

Fish stock

Clams

ESCABECHE

Fish cooked in aromatic vinegar

The Spanish developed the habit of marinating cooked fish in a vinegary mixture of vegetables to make sure the fish kept on long sea voyages — which may be why versions of this dish turn up in the Caribbean. Serves 6.

INGREDIENTS

salt and black pepper
1kg (2lb) fish fillets, such as sea bream,
sea bass, swordfish, tuna
flour, to dust
125ml (4fl oz) olive oil
4 bay leaves
1 lemon, sliced
6 sprigs parsley
2 large onions
6 cloves garlic, peeled
2 large carrots, peeled and thinly sliced
1 tsp sweet paprika
175ml (6fl oz) white wine vinegar
175ml (6fl oz) white wine

PREPARATION

1 Season the fish well then dust lightly with flour.
2 Heat the oil and when it is very hot add the fish. Fry for 4 minutes on each side until lightly golden. Remove the fish and place in an earthenware dish. Arrange the bay leaves, lemon and parsley on top.
3 Peel the onions, cut in half and slice into fine half-moons. Add the whole garlic cloves, carrot and onion to the remaining olive oil and fry over a low heat for 10 minutes until the onion is soft.
4 Add the paprika, seasoning, vinegar and wine and allow to bubble for 5 minutes. Take off the heat, add 90ml (3fl oz) of water and leave to cool.
5 Pour the cooled vinegar and vegetable mixture over the fish and leave for at least 24 hours. The fish will keep for up to a week in the refrigerator but should always be served at room temperature.

USKUMRU DOLMASI

Stuffed mackerel

It is said that the suitability of a Turkish wife was once measured by her ability to stuff a mackerel; whether you are a male or female cook, this is a dish that requires patience. Its feast-day origins are apparent in its richness and I prefer to serve it in small slices as a starter for 8 people. You need a needle and thread to sew the fish up after stuffing.

INGREDIENTS

4 small mackerel, ungutted, weighing
approximately 375g (12oz) each
30ml (2 tbsps) olive oil
1 large onion, finely chopped
2 cloves garlic, finely chopped
125g (4oz) chopped walnuts
60g (2oz) raisins
1 tsp cinnamon
2 cloves, ground
4 allspice berries, ground
good pinch of nutmeg
salt and black pepper
3 tbsps finely chopped fresh parsley
olive, sunflower or vegetable oil for deep-frying
2 large eggs, beaten
175g (6oz) dried breadcrumbs
4 lemons, quartered

PREPARATION

1 Remove the head of the mackerel. Pull the guts out through the cavity and discard them, taking care not to break the delicate skin.
2 Break the backbone of the mackerel and begin to work loose the flesh, as shown in step 1, opposite. Squeeze out the flesh, leaving the layer attached to the fish skin intact.
3 Warm the olive oil in a heavy frying pan over a low heat and add the onion and garlic. Stew gently for 10 minutes, until the onion is soft.
4 Stir in the flesh of the fish, the walnuts, raisins, spices and seasoning to taste. Cook the stuffing gently for a further 5 minutes, stirring continuously. Mix in the parsley and leave to cool.
5 When the stuffing is cool enough to handle, pack it into the fish skins, following steps 2–3, opposite.
6 Pour oil into a large pan to a depth of 2.5cm (1in) and heat gently.
7 Dip the fish first in the beaten egg and then in the breadcrumbs, making sure it is well coated. Fry in the oil for 5 minutes on either side.
8 Cut off the stitched end of the mackerel and discard. Cut the fish into slices and serve hot or cold with fresh lemon wedges.

STUFFING A MACKEREL

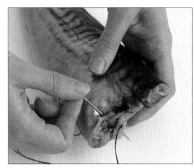

1 Bend back the fish at the tail end to break the backbone. Massage the fish with your thumbs to loosen the flesh, pull out the backbone and carefully squeeze out the flesh, picking out small bones.

2 Using a teaspoon, pack the stuffing into the cavity, pushing it as far down the tail as you can, but leaving a 1cm (½in) space at the head end.

3 Taking some strong thread and a darning needle, stitch the two sides of the head cavity together, being careful not to tear the skin.

SARDALYA SARMASI

Stuffed sardines in vine leaves

Turkish cooks have developed the skill of grilling fish over charcoal to something of an art form. But even they find it difficult to prevent sardines from breaking up on the barbecue, so first they wrap the fish in vine leaves. Illustrated on page 94.

INGREDIENTS

8 vine leaves in brine
8 sardines, scaled and gutted (see page 152)
4–6 tbsps finely chopped fresh coriander
4–6 tbsps finely chopped fresh parsley
4 cloves garlic, crushed and finely chopped
60ml (4 tbsps) olive oil
salt and black pepper
2 lemons, quartered, to serve

PREPARATION

1 Soak the vine leaves in water for 45 minutes, changing the water halfway through.
2 With a sharp knife, slit the sardines along the length of the belly. Hold them open, then press them flat and pull out the backbone. Pick over the flesh, removing any stray bones.
3 Combine the remaining ingredients, except the lemons, and stuff the fish with the mixture. Drain the vine leaves and wrap one around each fish.
4 Grill the fish, preferably over hot charcoal, for 3–5 minutes on each side. Serve with lemon.

CALAMARES RELLENOS

Stuffed squid

The shape of the body sac of the squid makes it ideal for stuffing. This Spanish recipe uses a savoury mixture of cured ham and rice. The stuffed squid are then gently simmered in a thick tomato sauce until meltingly tender.

INGREDIENTS

16 medium squid
175g (6oz) long-grain rice, rinsed and drained
90ml (3fl oz) olive oil
1 Spanish onion, finely chopped
4 cloves garlic, finely chopped
175g (6oz) chunk Serrano ham, finely chopped
2 tbsps chopped fresh parsley
1 tsp sweet paprika
salt and black pepper
1 tbsp tomato purée
750g (1½lb) plum tomatoes, skinned, deseeded and chopped
good pinch of sugar
1 sprig thyme
175ml (6fl oz) dry white wine

PREPARATION

1 Clean the squid (see page 153) then finely chop the tentacles, leaving the body whole.
2 Bring a large pan of salted water to the boil and boil the rice for 10 minutes. Drain and rinse well under cold water.
3 Heat half the oil in a frying pan and add half the onion and half the garlic. Cook gently for 10 minutes until the onion is soft. Turn up the heat to medium, add the chopped tentacles, ham, parsley, paprika and seasoning. Cook for 2 minutes, stirring all the time. Take off the heat and stir in the cooked rice.
4 Make a tomato sauce by heating 30ml (2 tbsps) of the remaining oil and frying the remainder of the onion and garlic over a low heat until soft, approximately 10 minutes. Add the tomato purée, chopped tomatoes, sugar, thyme and more seasoning. Cook for 5 minutes, until the tomatoes have broken down. Add the wine, cover and simmer for 15 minutes.
5 Preheat the oven to 160°C/325°F/gas 3. Stuff the squid bodies with the rice and ham mixture, taking care not to over-fill them.
6 Heat the remaining oil and gently fry the stuffed squid for 5 minutes, turning once, until they are lightly coloured but not browned. Using a slotted spoon, transfer them to an earthenware casserole, pour over the tomato sauce and cover.
7 Bake the squid in the preheated oven for 1 hour, until very tender. Serve piping hot.

TIAN DE SARDINES

Sardines baked with Swiss chard, spinach and Parmesan

The tian is a special earthenware gratin dish used in the region around Nice, and it has has lent its name to many recipes. In this version, the bubbling top of Parmesan cheese and green leaves hides a surprise filling of sardines. The Niçois also make this dish with the tiny transparent goby fish, or nounats.

INGREDIENTS

750g (1½lb) sardines, scaled, gutted and filleted
500g (1lb) Swiss chard leaves
750g (1½lb) baby spinach leaves
90ml (3fl oz) olive oil, plus oil to grease
2 cloves garlic
60g (2oz) long-grain rice, rinsed and drained
2 tbsps chopped fresh parsley
175g (6oz) freshly grated Parmesan
salt and black pepper
good pinch of nutmeg
4 large eggs, beaten
60g (2oz) fresh white breadcrumbs

PREPARATION

1 If you have to fillet the sardines yourself, follow step 2 of Sardalya Sarmasi, opposite. Do not worry if the fillets do not remain whole. The important thing is to remove all the bones.
2 Wash the Swiss chard and spinach, removing any stalks. Cut the leaves into fine strips and dry well.
3 In a heavy pan over a low heat, warm 30ml (2 tbsps) of oil with a peeled garlic clove. Add the Swiss chard and cook for 5 minutes, until the leaves have wilted and the liquid has evaporated. Set aside the Swiss chard and repeat the process with the spinach, using another 30ml (2 tbsps) of oil and the second whole peeled garlic clove.
4 Bring a large pan of salted water to the boil and cook the rice at a rolling boil for 15 minutes. Rinse under cold water and drain thoroughly.
5 Preheat the oven to 220°C/425°F/gas 7. Stir the cooked rice, Swiss chard and spinach, the parsley, 150g (5oz) of Parmesan, the seasoning and nutmeg into the beaten eggs.
6 Oil an earthenware gratin dish and put a 2.5cm (1in) layer of the rice mixture over the base. Layer the sardines on top and cover with the remainder of the rice mixture.
7 Mix together the remaining Parmesan and the breadcrumbs and sprinkle this mixture over the top. Finally, dribble the top with olive oil.
8 Bake the tian for 25 minutes, until the surface is browned and the contents bubbling. Serve very hot.

SAMAK CHARMOULA

Marinated and baked fish

There is no set recipe for this Moroccan marinade for fish – every cook has a favourite version. You can vary the spices according to your taste but the marinade should always be thick with herbs. The marinated fish can then be baked, grilled or used in tagines.

INGREDIENTS

4 cloves garlic
1 tsp salt
juice of 2 lemons
1½ tbsps ground cumin
1 tbsp sweet paprika
¼ tsp cayenne pepper
½ tsp black pepper
4 tbsps chopped fresh coriander
4 tbsps chopped fresh parsley
125ml (4fl oz) olive oil
1 large fish, such as grey mullet or sea bass, weighing 1.25kg (2½lb), scaled and gutted (see page 152)

PREPARATION

1 Using a pestle and mortar, crush the garlic cloves with the salt. In a food processor or blender, process the crushed garlic with all the ingredients apart from the oil and the fish until you have a paste.
2 Begin to add the oil in a slow stream, increasing the speed of the processor once the oil has amalgamated with the other ingredients.
3 Pour the mixture into a large pan and warm over a low heat for 1 minute to bring out the spicy aromas – do not allow the marinade to boil. Leave it to cool.
4 Wash the fish well inside and out. Make 4 deep diagonal slashes on each side of the fish then place it in an earthenware dish. Pour over the sauce and leave to marinate for 24 hours.
5 When you are ready to cook, preheat the oven to 180°C/350°F/gas 4. Cover the marinated fish with foil and bake for 45 minutes. Serve hot.

FISH PLAKI

Baked fish with vegetables

Though it can be hard these days in the Greek islands to lay your hands on a large fish, if you do it will probably have been cooked in this simple style, which is equally popular in neighbouring Turkey.

INGREDIENTS

4 carrots, peeled
4 sticks celery
1 onion
1 green pepper, cored and deseeded
2 large potatoes, peeled
175ml (6fl oz) olive oil
salt and black pepper
1 large fish, such as sea bream, weighing approximately
1.25kg (2½lb) or 4 small fish, such as small grey mullet,
scaled and gutted (see page 152) or 4 fish steaks
4 cloves garlic, finely chopped
2 tbsps tomato purée
¼ tsp cayenne pepper
1 lemon, sliced, to garnish
parsley sprigs, to garnish

PREPARATION

1 Cut the carrots across into slices 1cm (½in) thick. Cut the celery into 2.5cm (1in) pieces. Chop the onion into quarters and then into fine slices. Cut the pepper into fine strips. Cut the potatoes across into slices 1cm (½in) thick. Wash and drain all the vegetables thoroughly.

2 In a large heavy pan with a lid, gently heat the oil. Add the vegetables, season well, cover and leave to cook over a low heat for 30 minutes (they should be quite soft).

3 Preheat the oven to 200°C/400°F/gas 6.

4 Remove the vegetables from the oil with a slotted spoon. Lay the fish in an earthenware dish and carefully arrange the vegetables around and over it.

5 Fry the garlic for 1 minute in the oil in which the vegetables were cooked, then add the tomato purée, salt to taste and cayenne pepper. Cook for a further 3 minutes, stirring all the time.

6 Carefully pour in 1 litre (1¼ pints) of water. Bring to the boil, then pour the liquid over the fish and vegetables, making sure you scrape all the garlic out of the pan.

7 Bake the dish uncovered in the oven for 30–45 minutes, depending on the size of fish, until the fish is very tender (Turkish cooks often prefer to cook fish for longer).

8 Leave the fish to cool in its liquid and serve at room temperature, garnished with slices of lemon and sprigs of parsley.

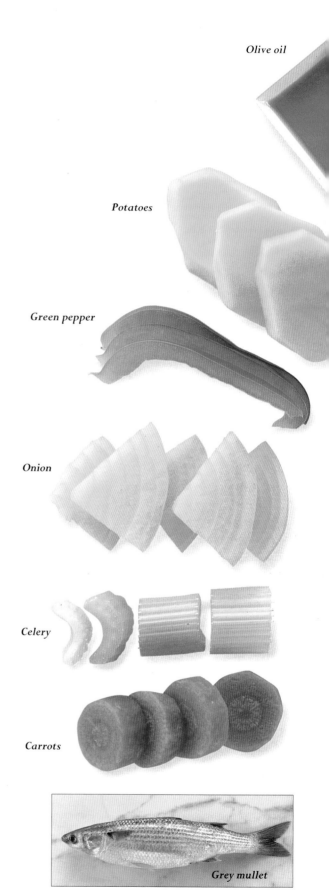

Olive oil

Potatoes

Green pepper

Onion

Celery

Carrots

Grey mullet

Salt

Black
pepper

Garlic

Tomato
purée

Cayenne
pepper

Lemon

Parsley

MEAT DISHES

Mediterranean cooks are economical by nature: meat is often used in only small quantities to enhance the flavour of vegetable dishes and all parts of the animal are used, with delicious results. Cured meats and sausages play an important role and, in season, game is frequently found on the table. The most commonly offered meats are pork in the west of the region, lamb in the east and poultry throughout. On feast days, meat dishes always take a centre stage – a whole lamb roasted on the spit is a particular speciality.

DJEJ MESHWI

Moroccan grilled spring chicken

Illustrated on page 50.

INGREDIENTS

4 spring chickens
90ml (3fl oz) olive oil
juice of 2 lemons
4 cloves garlic, crushed and finely chopped
1 tsp black pepper
sea salt
2 tbsps chopped fresh parsley
2 lemons, quartered, to serve

PREPARATION

1 Spatchcock the chickens (see page 155).
2 Mix together the olive oil, lemon juice, garlic and pepper and rub this marinade all over the chickens, slipping some between the skin and the flesh. Leave the chickens to marinate for several hours, turning them regularly.
3 Grill the chickens, preferably over charcoal, skin-side down. Cook until the skin is nicely browned, about 10 minutes. Turn the chickens over, sprinkle with plenty of salt and brush with the marinade. Cook for a further 10 minutes, then turn over again and cook for a final 5 minutes to crisp the skin. Sprinkle with parsley and serve with little bowls of coarse sea salt and lemon quarters.

ŞIŞ KÖFTESI

Turkish minced meat on skewers

Illustrated on page 50.

INGREDIENTS

1 large onion
750g (1½lb) minced lamb, preferably from the shoulder
2 cloves garlic, finely chopped
4 tbsps chopped fresh parsley or coriander
1 tsp sweet paprika
1 tsp ground cumin
good pinch of cayenne pepper
1 tsp salt
½ tsp black pepper
2 lemons, quartered, to serve

PREPARATION

1 Grate the onion – be careful to catch the juices.
2 Blend all the ingredients except the lemons in the food processor until you have a smooth paste. Leave the mixture in a bowl for at least 30 minutes for the flavours to mingle.
3 Dampen your hands and take an egg-sized piece of the meat mixture and fashion it into a long thin sausage shape on the skewer (see page 155). Continue until all the mixture is used up.
4 Grill the kebabs, preferably over charcoal, for 6–7 minutes, turning them frequently to brown them evenly. Serve with lemon quarters.

YOĞURTLU KEBAB

Lamb kebabs with yogurt

This Turkish dish, popular throughout the eastern Mediterranean, adds fresh tomato sauce, yogurt, bread and pine kernels to the smoky morsels of lamb, making the dish a complete meal.

INGREDIENTS

750g (1½lb) lamb, preferably from the shoulder, cut into 2.5cm (1in) cubes
45ml (3 tbsps) olive oil
750g (1½lb) plum tomatoes, skinned, deseeded and chopped
salt and black pepper
pinch of sugar, optional
2 pitta or other flat breads
300ml (½ pint) thick natural yogurt, at room temperature
30g (1oz) pine kernels
1 tsp sweet paprika
1 tbsp chopped fresh parsley, to serve
MARINADE
1 mild onion, grated
juice of 1 lemon
30ml (2 tbsps) olive oil
2 cloves garlic, crushed
1 tsp ground cumin
½ tsp sweet paprika
1 sprig fresh thyme
salt and black pepper

PREPARATION

1 Mix together all the marinade ingredients and pour over the lamb. Marinate for at least 2 hours, turning the meat once or twice.
2 Heat 30ml (1 tbsp) of oil in a pan and add the tomato flesh. Sweat gently for 10 minutes, stirring regularly, until the tomatoes have broken down and formed a thick sauce. Remove from the heat and season, adding a pinch of sugar if the tomatoes are not sweet enough.
3 Remove the meat from the marinade and thread on skewers. Grill, preferably over charcoal, for a minimum of 4–5 minutes on each side.
4 While the meat is cooking, split the breads in half lengthways and toast until lightly browned on both sides. Break the toasted bread into squares and scatter over the base of the serving dish. Spread the tomato sauce over the bread.
5 Lay the kebabs on top of the tomato sauce and cover them with yogurt. Briefly toast the pine kernels until golden.
6 Warm the remaining oil and stir in the paprika. Pour the oil over the yogurt and scatter with the pine kernels and parsley.

ŞIŞ KEBAB

Turkish lamb kebabs

Illustrated on page 51.

INGREDIENTS

750g (1½lb) lamb, preferably from the shoulder, cut into 2.5cm (1in) cubes
1 mild onion, grated
juice of 1 lemon
30ml (2 tbsps) olive oil
2 cloves garlic, crushed
2 bay leaves
salt and black pepper
1 tbsp chopped parsley, to serve

PREPARATION

1 Mix together the onion, lemon juice, oil, garlic, bay leaves and a generous amount of seasoning. Pour this mixture over the lamb. Marinate for at least 2 hours, turning the meat once or twice.
2 Remove the meat from the marinade and thread on skewers. Grill, preferably over charcoal, for a minimum of 4–5 minutes on both sides. Serve scattered with chopped parsley.

PINCHOS MORUNOS

Spanish pork kebabs

Illustrated on page 38.

INGREDIENTS

625g (1¼lb) pork escalopes
1 tsp ground cumin
1 tsp sweet paprika
½ tsp cayenne pepper, or more to taste
1 dried bay leaf, crumbled
½ tsp dried thyme
90ml (3fl oz) olive oil
2 lemons, quartered, and sea salt, to serve

PREPARATION

1 Trim any fat from the pork and cut the meat into 1.5cm (¾in) cubes.
2 Mix together the spices, herbs and oil to make a marinade and pour it over the pork, making sure every piece is well coated. Leave to marinate for at least 4 hours, preferably overnight.
3 Thread 2 or 3 cubes on small kebab sticks. Cook over charcoal or under a medium grill for 8–10 minutes, turning the kebabs and basting frequently with the marinade. Serve with lemon quarters and sea salt.

FOIE DE VEAU AUX CÂPRES

Calves' liver in tomato sauce with capers

Much of the cooking of the Mediterranean has a rough and ready feel, but this is undeniably a luxury dish. Thin slices of calves' liver just flashed in the pan then bathed in a deep red tomato sauce flecked with the green of capers and parsley are a favourite in Provence.

INGREDIENTS

375g (12oz) calves' liver, cut into very thin slices
15ml (1 tbsp) olive oil
1 tbsp chopped fresh parsley
TOMATO AND CAPER SAUCE
30ml (2 tbsps) extra-virgin olive oil
750g (1½lb) juicy plum tomatoes, skinned and chopped
1 tsp tomato purée
good pinch of sugar
salt and black pepper
250ml (8fl oz) dry white wine
2 tbsps capers, rinsed and drained

PREPARATION

1 First make the sauce. Heat the extra-virgin olive oil in a heavy pan and add the tomatoes, tomato purée, sugar and seasoning. Cook over a low heat for 10 minutes, stirring regularly, until the tomatoes have broken down.
2 Add the wine, bring to the boil and turn down to a simmer. Leave to cook uncovered for 30 minutes, until you have a thick sauce.
3 Add the capers to the tomato sauce and check for seasoning – it should be quite peppery with plenty of bite.
4 To cook the liver, choose a large pan in which all the slices will lie flat. Heat the olive oil over a high heat and when it is nearly spitting add the liver. Provided it is cut fine enough, it should need no more than 30 seconds' cooking on either side.
5 Transfer the liver to a warmed serving plate. Pour the tomato sauce into the pan in which the liver was cooked and swirl it round to amalgamate the oil. Pour the sauce over the liver, sprinkle with parsley and serve.

RIÑONES AL JEREZ

Kidneys cooked in sherry

In Spain this dish is often prepared using veal kidneys, but the much smaller lambs' kidneys are a good substitute. Riñones al Jerez can be served as part of a selection of tapas, but the proportions given here are for an ultra-rapid main course, to be served with rice and a green salad.

INGREDIENTS

30ml (2 tbsps) olive oil
12 lambs' kidneys, washed, cored and quartered
2 cloves garlic, finely chopped
150ml (¼ pint) fino sherry
salt and black pepper

PREPARATION

1 Heat the oil in a heavy pan over a high heat. When the oil is very hot, add the kidneys and garlic and fry for 2 minutes, stirring continuously.
2 Stand back and add the sherry – be careful as it will spit. Season and cook over a high heat for a further minute. Serve immediately.

LA PIZZAIOLA

Steak with tomato sauce

Few recipes could be simpler than the pizzaiola of southern Italy, yet have such a dramatic result. In minutes a potentially disappointing steak can be transformed into a dish redolent with the Mediterranean flavours of olive oil, tomato, herbs and garlic.

INGREDIENTS

salt and black pepper
4 thinly cut steaks, each weighing 125–150g (4–5oz)
45ml (3 tbsps) olive oil
3 cloves garlic
4 ripe plum tomatoes, skinned, deseeded and chopped or 425g (14oz) can whole peeled tomatoes, chopped
2 tsps chopped fresh oregano or ½ tsp dried oregano

PREPARATION

1 Season the steaks well. Heat the oil in a heavy frying pan until it is nearly spitting. Add the steaks and fry for 30 seconds on each side to seal them. Remove the steaks from the oil and set aside.
2 Add the garlic to the oil in the pan and as soon as it starts to sizzle add the tomatoes, oregano and seasoning to taste. Allow to simmer for 5 minutes, stirring continuously.
3 Return the steaks to the pan and cook for 5 minutes, turning them once.

SOUMANATE BI' LEINAB

Quail with grapes

This elegant recipe from Morocco is a simple but delicious way of preparing quail. It is best made with slightly under-ripe white grapes. Similar recipes for partridges are found over the water in Andalusia.

INGREDIENTS

60g (2oz) butter
8 quail
375g (12oz) seedless white grapes
salt and black pepper
1 tsp ground ginger

PREPARATION

1 Melt the butter over a low heat in a heavy frying pan just large enough to take all the birds lying flat. Add the quail and fry for 10 minutes, turning regularly, until they are lightly browned.
2 Meanwhile, purée three-quarters of the grapes in a food processor. Strain the resulting pulp, reserving the juice.
3 Season the quail and sprinkle over the ginger. Add the grape juice, turn the quail breast-side down, cover and cook over a low heat for 10 minutes.
4 Slice the remaining grapes in half and add to the pan. Turn the birds breast-side up and leave to cook for a further 3–4 minutes, until the grapes are warmed through.

ALBONDIGAS

Pork and parsley meatballs

Fried balls of minced pork studded with parsley and flavoured with garlic and spices are a favourite tapa *in Spain. Served with a fresh tomato sauce, they also make a delicious main course.*

INGREDIENTS

1 small onion
500g (1lb) finely minced pork, preferably from the loin
60g (2oz) white breadcrumbs
60g (2oz) finely chopped fresh parsley
2 cloves garlic, minced
1 tsp sweet paprika
pinch of freshly grated nutmeg
pinch of cayenne pepper
2 large eggs
salt and black pepper
sunflower or vegetable oil for frying
flour, to dust

PREPARATION

1 Mince the onion, being careful to catch the juices. Mix together the pork, onion, breadcrumbs, parsley, garlic, paprika, nutmeg, cayenne pepper, one egg and plenty of seasoning. Break off walnut-sized pieces and shape into balls.
2 Pour oil to a depth of 1cm (½in) into a frying pan and warm over a medium heat.
3 Roll the meatballs in seasoned flour. Beat the remaining egg. When the oil is nearly smoking, dip each ball into the egg and then lower it into the hot oil to seal it. Reduce the heat and leave to cook for 10 minutes.
4 Turn the meatballs over and cook slowly for another 10 minutes, or until they are cooked through. Turn the heat up at the end of cooking to crisp the meatballs – they should be golden.
5 Drain the meatballs on kitchen paper and serve hot or cold with Allioli (see page 66).

DAOUD PASHA

Spicy lamb meatballs with pine kernels in tomato sauce

Meatballs cooked over charcoal or poached in a sauce are a distinctive feature of the cooking of the eastern Mediterranean. In this Syrian dish they are studded with pine kernels and cooked in a lemon-sharp tomato sauce.

INGREDIENTS

¼ tsp ground cumin
¼ tsp ground cinnamon
¼ tsp ground coriander
½ tsp black pepper
60g (2oz) pine kernels
625g (1¼lb) finely minced lamb
2 onions
30ml (2 tbsps) olive oil
60g (2oz) tomato purée
juice of 1 lemon
salt
2 tbsps chopped fresh parsley or coriander, to serve

PREPARATION

1 Mix the spices and pine kernels into the lamb. Break off walnut-sized pieces and shape into balls.
2 Peel the onions, cut in half and slice into fine half-moons. Choose a large deep frying pan and slowly heat the oil. Add the onion and fry gently for 20 minutes over a low heat, stirring from time to time. The onion should be soft but not coloured.
3 Add the meatballs to the pan and fry gently, shaking the pan occasionally. After 5 minutes the meatballs should be lightly coloured all over.
4 Beat together the tomato purée and lemon juice and add sufficient water to make 500ml (16fl oz). Pour this mixture into the pan, add salt to taste and leave to simmer for 20 minutes, turning the meatballs halfway through cooking.
5 Check the seasoning of the sauce, sprinkle the dish with parsley and serve hot.

ARNI FRIKASE AVGOLEMONO

Fricassee of lamb with egg and lemon sauce

Avgolemono, the sharp egg and lemon sauce beloved of the Greeks, marries especially well with their favourite meat, lamb. Traditionally the meat is slowly stewed before the final addition of the sauce, but I find this quick version very satisfactory for a simple summer lunch. Illustrated on page 112.

INGREDIENTS

625g (1¼lb) boneless lamb fillet
salt and black pepper
1 bunch spring onions
1 cos lettuce
30ml (2 tbsps) olive oil
350ml (12fl oz) light lamb stock (see page 155)
3 egg yolks
juice of 2 lemons
1 tbsp chopped fresh dill

PREPARATION

1 Cut the lamb into bite-sized pieces, approximately 2.5cm (1in) square, trimming off any fat. Season the chunks of meat well.
2 Roughly chop the spring onions, including the green part. Remove the heart of the lettuce, discarding the large outer leaves. Wash the heart well and chop into 1cm (½in) wide strips.
3 Heat the oil in a large frying pan over a medium heat. Add the spring onion and lamb and fry for 2 minutes, turning the meat regularly until it is browned all over.
4 Add the lettuce and the lamb stock, bring rapidly to the boil, then reduce the heat to low. Simmer gently for 5 minutes.
5 Meanwhile, beat the egg yolks with the lemon juice in a bowl. After the stock has simmered for 5 minutes, drain off the hot liquid from the frying pan and pour it into the egg and lemon mixture, whisking all the time to prevent the egg from curdling. Put the lamb and lettuce in a serving dish and keep warm in a low oven.
6 Turn the heat down as low as it will go and return the liquid to the pan. Simmer for 2–3 minutes, whisking continuously, until the sauce thickens slightly – on no account allow the liquid to return to the boil or it will curdle.
7 Take the pan off the heat, stir in the dill and add further seasoning to taste. Pour the sauce over the lamb and lettuce. Serve immediately.

POULET SAUTE AUX HERBES DE PROVENCE

Chicken sautéed with scrub herbs and garlic in white wine

As this dish cooks, it gives off those aromas that remind me of the Mediterranean – pungent garlic frying in fruity olive oil, the fragrance of herbs and the headiness of wine in the pan. This is a basic recipe for chicken, but you'll find plenty of regional variations. Accompany with a green salad. Illustrated on page 112.

INGREDIENTS

3 fat cloves garlic
30ml (2 tbsps) olive oil
1 chicken, jointed (see page 154), or 8 small chicken thighs and drumsticks
a few sprigs each of fresh thyme, oregano and rosemary
250ml (8fl oz) dry white wine
salt and black pepper
juice of ½ lemon

PREPARATION

1 Peel the garlic and chop the cloves into quarters.
2 Heat the oil in a deep heavy frying pan large enough to take all the chicken pieces. Add the chicken, garlic and herbs and fry briskly for 5 minutes, turning the chicken to brown it lightly.
3 Pour in the wine, bring to the boil and turn down to a simmer. Add seasoning, cover and leave to cook for 30 minutes, turning the chicken pieces halfway through cooking.
4 Finish with the lemon juice and serve very hot. The chicken should be tender and the sauce syrupy.

ARNI FRIKASE AVGOLEMONO
Fricassee of lamb with egg
and lemon sauce
(page 111)

ARROSTA DI MAIALE
Roast pork Italian style
(page 114)

**POULET SAUTE AUX HERBES
DE PROVENCE**
Chicken sautéed with scrub herbs
and garlic in white wine
(page 111)

MOUSSAKA
Baked aubergines layered with lamb

Most moussakas served today are quite unlike the Greek original, with its plump aubergines, spiced lamb in a rich sauce and a light cheese custard, layered and baked until the flavours meld together. Served with bread and a green salad, it is a satisfying meal. Serves 6–8.

INGREDIENTS

1kg (2lb) aubergines
salt
2 white onions, finely chopped
olive oil for frying
750g (1½lb) minced lamb
1 tsp ground cinnamon
1 tsp ground allspice
black pepper
250ml (8fl oz) red wine
1kg (2lb) plum tomatoes, skinned, deseeded and chopped
1 tsp tomato purée
1 tsp honey
4 tbsps chopped fresh parsley
1 tbsp dried oregano (rigani)
125ml (4fl oz) lamb or chicken stock (see page 155)
500ml (16fl oz) full-fat milk
125g (4oz) curd cheese
90g (3oz) feta cheese
3 large whole eggs, plus 3 egg yolks
pinch of freshly grated nutmeg
60g (2oz) white breadcrumbs
60g (2oz) freshly grated Greek hard cheese or Parmesan

PREPARATION

1 Wash the aubergines and cut them into 5mm (¼in) slices. Salt and blot them (see page 150).
2 Stew the onions gently in 45ml (3 tbsps) of oil for 15 minutes, until soft but not coloured. Turn up the heat and add the lamb, spices and seasoning. Cook over a high heat for 5 minutes, stirring continuously, until the meat is browned all over.
3 Pour in the wine and allow to bubble for 5 minutes. Add the tomatoes, tomato purée and honey, turn down to a simmer and leave to cook uncovered for 10 minutes, stirring occasionally to help the tomatoes break down.
4 Add the herbs and stock and simmer gently for 30 minutes, until the sauce is very thick.
5 Process or beat together the milk and the curd and feta cheeses. Add the eggs and egg yolks, and beat well. Stir in the nutmeg.
6 Heat this mixture in a double boiler (see page 156) over gently simmering water for 15–20 minutes, stirring continuously, until the custard thickens – do not allow it to boil or it will curdle.

7 Take a non-stick frying pan, pour in just enough oil to cover the base and place over a medium heat. When the oil is very hot, add the rinsed and dried aubergine slices. Fry for 1 minute on each side, then drain on kitchen paper. Repeat, adding more oil if necessary, until all the aubergines are cooked.
8 Preheat the oven to 180°C/350°F/gas 4. Choose a large deep baking dish. Assemble the moussaka, starting with a layer of aubergine, following with lamb, cheese custard, more aubergine, lamb, aubergine again and finishing with cheese custard.
9 Mix together the breadcrumbs and grated cheese and sprinkle over the top. Bake for 1 hour, until the top is crispy and the contents bubbling.

ARROSTA DI MAIALE
Roast pork Italian style

The Italian love affair with pork reaches its height with porchetta, roast stuffed suckling pig. Fennel is an essential ingredient of its stuffing, and it is also used with smaller roasts, as here. The wine in the roasting tin ensures the meat is moist, though you will get no crackling. Serves 6. Illustrated on page 113.

INGREDIENTS

3 cloves garlic
salt
3 bulbs fennel, fronds attached
½ tsp fennel seeds
60ml (4 tbsps) olive oil
1 bottle white wine (approximately)
1.5 –1.75kg (3–3½lb) pork leg joint, on the bone
black pepper
1 sprig rosemary
90ml (3fl oz) Marsala, optional

PREPARATION

1 Preheat the oven to 180°C/350°F/gas 4.
2 Crush the garlic cloves with a little salt. Remove the fennel fronds and chop roughly. Using a food processor, process the garlic, fennel seeds and fronds, oil, and 125ml (4fl oz) wine to make a paste.
3 Make incisions in the pork and smear with paste. Season with pepper and place in a small roasting tin. Surround with halved fennel bulbs. Pour in wine to a depth of 1.5cm (¾in). Add the rosemary and cook for 30 minutes.
4 Reduce the heat to 160°C/325°F/gas 3 and cook for 2–2½ hours, basting with the pan juices.
5 Remove the pork and fennel and allow to sit for 10 minutes. Skim the fat from the tin and add the Marsala or a glass of wine. Place over a high heat, reduce to a syrupy sauce, and pour over the pork.

PATO A LA SEVILLANA

Duck with olives, orange and sherry

This recipe brings together three of the culinary treasures of Andalusia – the bone dry sherry, with its tang of salt, green olives and sweet juicy oranges.

INGREDIENTS

1 duck weighing 2kg (4lb)
2 oranges
3 cloves garlic
1 onion, chopped
1 carrot, chopped
125g (4oz) green olives
250ml (8fl oz) fino sherry
4 peppercorns
2 bay leaves
2 sprigs fresh thyme
salt and black pepper

PREPARATION

1 Preheat the oven to 180°C/325°F/gas 3.
2 Prick the duck all over with a fork. Place a halved orange and 1 unpeeled garlic clove inside the bird. Roast the bird breast-side down on a wire rack over a pan for 30 minutes.
3 After the duck has cooked for 30 minutes, drain off the fat. Turn it breast side-up and roast for a further 15 minutes.
4 Meanwhile, gently fry the onion, carrot and remaining garlic, finely chopped, in a tablespoon of the reserved duck fat, until very soft. Add 350ml (12fl oz) of water and simmer for 30 minutes to make a stock. Add the olives to the stock for the last 5 minutes.
5 Remove the duck from the oven and cut it into 4 pieces. Place the duck in a casserole. Pour over the sherry, the contents of the stock pan and the juice of the remaining orange. Add the peppercorns, bay leaves, thyme and seasoning.
6 Bring to the boil, turn down to a simmer, cover and leave to cook on a low heat for 45 minutes. Remove the thyme before serving.

CAPRIOLO IN AGRODOLCE

Venison in a sour and sweet sauce

The Romans were very fond of sauces made with honey and vinegar; the chocolate in this sauce is a later addition. Hare and wild boar are also cooked in this way.

INGREDIENTS

750g (1½lb) venison stewing steak
1 large onion, chopped
2 large carrots, chopped
2 sticks celery, chopped
4 garlic cloves, peeled and crushed
bouquet garni made up of 1 fresh bay leaf and 2 sprigs each of fresh rosemary and thyme
black pepper
6 juniper berries
60ml (4 tbsps) olive oil
150ml (¼ pint) red wine vinegar
300ml (½ pint) red wine
salt
flour, to dust
60g (2oz) dark bitter chocolate, grated
1 tbsp honey
2 tbsps chopped fresh parsley

PREPARATION

1 Trim the venison and cut into large pieces.
2 Place the pieces of venison in a bowl with the onion, carrots and celery. Add the garlic and bouquet garni, plenty of pepper and the juniper berries. Pour over half the oil, 30ml (2 tbsps) of vinegar and all the wine. Leave to marinate for at least 4 hours, preferably overnight.
3 Preheat the oven to 140°C/275°F/gas 1, if using (see step 5). Remove the venison from the marinade and pat dry. Season the flour and dust the venison. Heat the remaining oil in a pan and brown the meat.
4 Remove the meat from the pan and set aside. Strain the vegetable marinade, reserving the liquid, and heat the vegetables in the pan for 5 minutes.
5 Bring the marinade to the boil in a small saucepan. Add the chocolate, stirring to melt it. Return the meat to the pan, pour over the hot marinade and, if necessary, enough water to cover it. Cover the pan with aluminium foil and then with the lid. Place over a very low heat, so that the liquid is barely simmering, and cook for 2½–3 hours. Alternatively, cook in the preheated oven for 3 hours.
6 Just before serving, make a syrup by mixing the honey with 30ml (2 tbsps) of water over a low heat. Stir in the remaining vinegar and allow to bubble for 2 minutes. Add this mixture to the pan.
7 Check the seasoning and balance of flavour – add more vinegar, if desired – then sprinkle with parsley.

DAUBE DE BOEUF
Beef casserole

This classic Provençal dish is not for a cook in a hurry. Traditionally the daube was left to simmer on the stove all day, so that by evening the kitchen would be filled with the powerful scent of wine and herbs. The slower and longer the dish cooks, the better it will taste. You can, if you like, cut down the marinating time, although the flavour will not be so intense. Daube tastes even better if made a day in advance. Serves 6–8.

Beef shin

Streaky bacon

Salt pork

Onions

Garlic

Black pepper

Ground allspice

Bouquet garni

Red wine

INGREDIENTS

1.5kg (3lb) shin or chuck of beef
2 onions, quartered
3 cloves garlic, peeled and crushed
black pepper
pinch of ground allspice
large bouquet garni made up of 4 sprigs each of fresh thyme and rosemary, 1 bay leaf and orange zest
600ml (1 pint) robust red wine
30ml (2 tbsps) olive oil
250g (8oz) salt pork
6 rashers smoked streaky bacon or 2 pieces pork rind
2 large carrots, thickly sliced
500g (1lb) plum tomatoes, skinned and quartered
125g (4oz) small black olives, preferably niçoise
60g (2oz) dried ceps or 250g (8oz) fresh wild mushrooms
salt
90g (3oz) per person fresh noodles, such as tagliatelle

PREPARATION

1 The day before you want to cook the daube, trim the fat from the beef and discard. Cut the meat into large pieces and place in a bowl with the onion, garlic, spices, bouquet garni, wine and oil. Leave to marinate, preferably for 24 hours.
2 The next day, cut the salt pork into lardons (see page 156). Place in a large pan together with the rashers of bacon and cover with water. Bring slowly to the boil and boil for 5 minutes. Drain.
3 Line the base of an earthenware or cast-iron pot with half the bacon or one piece of pork rind.
4 Drain the beef, reserving the marinade. Place the beef, onion, garlic, bouquet garni and lardons in the pan, interspersing with carrots and tomatoes.
5 Bring the marinade to the boil and pour it over the meat. Lay the remaining bacon or pork rind over the beef. Cover the pan with greaseproof paper or aluminium foil and then with the lid.
6 Cook the daube for 3½–4 hours, either gently simmering on the stove or in a low oven (140°C/275°F/gas 1). Meanwhile, blanch the olives for 2 minutes in boiling water. Soak the ceps in a little warm water for 15 minutes, then drain.

7 After the daube has cooked for 3 hours, add the olives and ceps. Replace the lid and cook for a further 30 minutes, until the meat is tender enough to cut with a spoon.
8 Just before serving, bring 4 litres (7 pints) of salted water to the boil and add the fresh noodles. Cook until *al dente* (see page 156), then drain.
9 Skim the surface fat from the daube, discard the bacon and check for salt. Serve with the noodles.

Olive oil

Noodles

Carrots

Tomatoes

Niçoise
olives

Dried ceps

Salt

117

TAGINE D'AGNEAU AUX ABRICOTS

Moroccan tagine of lamb with apricots

Tagines often contain dried or fresh fruit — those with quince or apricots are my favourites. This rich lamb tagine is delicious accompanied by flat bread to mop up the fragrant juices. Serves 4–6.

INGREDIENTS

1kg (2lb) shoulder of lamb, off the bone
2 large onions
1 tsp ground ginger
½ tsp black pepper
½ tsp ground cinnamon
good pinch of saffron
45g (1½oz) butter
salt
1 bunch coriander
250g (8oz) dried apricots

PREPARATION

1 Trim the meat of all fat and cut into large bite-sized pieces. Place the meat in a heavy casserole.

2 Grate one of the onions, being careful to catch the juices, and add to the casserole along with the spices, butter, a good pinch of salt and half the coriander tied in a bunch. Pour over 500ml (16fl oz) of water, bring to the boil, turn down to a simmer and leave to cook for 1 hour.

3 If you have ready-to-use dried apricots, there is no need to pre-soak them. Other varieties should be soaked for 1 hour in a little hot water, and then drained.

4 Finely chop the remaining onion. Remove the stalks from the rest of the coriander and roughly chop the leaves. After an hour add these to the casserole and cook for 30 minutes longer.

5 Add the apricots to the casserole and cook for a further 15–20 minutes, until they have plumped up. Check the seasoning and serve.

OSSOBUCO

Stewed shin of veal

This famous dish comes from the north of Italy, the cattle-rearing country, though the treatment of the main ingredient has distinctly southern influences. The final spiking with the gremolada, a mix of lemon, herbs and garlic, gives the dish enough bite to cheer up the greyest Milanese day.

INGREDIENTS

1–1.25kg (2–2½lb) shin of veal,
in 4 thick slices on the marrow bone
salt and black pepper
flour, to dust
30ml (2 tbsps) olive oil
30g (1oz) butter
2 large carrots, roughly chopped
2 onions, roughly chopped
4 sticks celery, roughly chopped
750g (1½lb) plum tomatoes, skinned, deseeded and
chopped
300ml (½ pint) dry white wine
300ml (½ pint) veal or light beef stock (see page 155)
2 tsps tomato purée
bouquet garni made up of 1 fresh bay leaf and 2 sprigs
each of fresh thyme, parsley, rosemary and a piece of
lemon zest

GREMOLADA

zest of ½ lemon, preferably unwaxed
2 cloves garlic, very finely chopped
2 tbsps chopped fresh parsley
2 sage leaves, finely chopped
½ tsp finely chopped rosemary needles

PREPARATION

1 Lightly dust the pieces of veal with seasoned flour. Heat the oil and butter in a pan in which all the slices will fit upright and briefly fry the veal until lightly browned on all sides.
2 Remove the meat from the pan and add the carrot, onion and celery. Cook gently in the fat until soft but not coloured. Return the meat to the pan, upright, and pour over the tomatoes.
3 Preheat the oven to 150°C/300°F/gas 2.
4 Mix together the wine, stock and tomato purée, bring to the boil in a separate saucepan and pour this hot mixture over the veal. Add seasoning and tuck in the bouquet garni. Cover the pan and cook in the preheated oven for 2½–3 hours, until the veal is very tender.
5 Meanwhile, make the gremolada. Finely grate the lemon zest and mix together with the garlic, parsley, sage and rosemary. Stir this mixture into the dish 5 minutes before serving.

CASSOULET

Haricot beans cooked with pork and duck

This peasant dish from the Languedoc gains its distinctive flavour from the use of goose or duck confit. Serves 6–8.

INGREDIENTS

500g (1lb) dried haricot beans, soaked overnight
bouquet garni made up of 1 fresh bay leaf and 2 sprigs
each of fresh parsley, rosemary, thyme and fennel
3 onions
4 cloves
2 carrots, peeled and halved
5 cloves garlic
8 black peppercorns
250g (8oz) piece of belly pork
125g (4oz) piece of pancetta or petit salé (see page 22)
4 pieces confit de canard (duck) or confit d'oie (goose) or
½ large duck, jointed
30ml (2 tbsps) olive oil
500g (1lb) Toulouse sausages or other 100% pork sausages
500g (1lb) dried garlic sausages or chorizo
500g (1lb) plum tomatoes, skinned, deseeded and chopped
salt and black pepper

PREPARATION

1 Put the beans in a large heavy pan and cover with 2.5 litres (4 pints) of water. Add the bouquet garni, an onion studded with the cloves, the carrots, 2 garlic cloves and the peppercorns.
2 Tie the belly pork into a tight round and add to the pan with the pancetta. Bring to the boil and skim off any scum. Reduce the heat, cover and simmer until the beans are soft but still whole, 1–1½ hours.
3 Meanwhile, gently heat the pieces of confit in a heavy pan to release the fat. Alternatively, if using half a duck, prick the skin all over and then fry the pieces over a low heat, skin side-down, until the fat runs. In each instance, drain off and reserve the fat. Set aside the pieces of duck or goose.
4 Heat the oil in a frying pan and finely chop the remaining onions and garlic. Fry for 10 minutes, then remove with a slotted spoon and set aside.
5 Preheat the oven to 140°C/275°F/gas 1. Drain the beans and remove the bouquet garni, clove-studded onion, garlic, belly pork and pancetta.
6 Take an earthenware casserole and fill it with layers of beans, onion, confit, sausages and tomatoes, seasoning as you go. Finish with a layer of beans.
7 Cook the cassoulet in the preheated oven for 2 hours, then dot with the reserved duck or goose fat. Increase the heat to 180°C/350°F/gas 4 and remove the lid. When the cassoulet has formed a crust, about 30 minutes, stir this back into the beans, then cook for a final 30 minutes.

PASTA, RICE AND GRAINS

Bread is a central element of the daily diet; no meal is complete without it. Then there are the myriad grain and pasta dishes: the bulgur wheat and couscous of the eastern Mediterranean and North Africa respectively; pilavs, paellas and risottos; pasta soups and baked pastas. Nor is pasta confined to Italy – there are versions in Provence, Catalonia and Turkey. These staples of the Mediterranean kitchen are not only nutritionally rich, they are also highly versatile foods that star in both simple everyday meals and some of the most sumptuous classics of the region.

BRUSCHETTA

Garlic bread

Though bruschetta is now interpreted as being bread topped with just about anything that takes the cook's fancy, in its original form it is simply garlic bread. Not just any garlic bread though – it should be slices of the best country bread, rubbed with juicy garlic, slaked with the best fruity green olive oil and sprinkled with salt and pepper.

INGREDIENTS

4 thick slices country-style Italian bread, preferably wholemeal sourdough bread
4 fat cloves garlic, peeled and halved
extra-virgin olive oil
salt and black pepper

PREPARATION

1 Grill the bread lightly on both sides (traditionally it is cooked over a wood-burning fire to give it a smoky flavour). Alternatively, bake it in a medium oven until crisp.
2 Rub one side of each slice of bread with the cut side of the garlic pieces.
3 Lay the bread on serving plates and dribble over a generous amount of olive oil. There should be just enough to soak through the bread. Season well and serve immediately.

PANZANELLA

Bread and tomato salad

In Catalonia they rub ripe tomatoes on bread and call it Pa amb Tomàquet. In southern Italy they go further and make a bread and tomato salad, as here. For best results, the tomatoes should have ripened in the sun.

INGREDIENTS

4 thick slices slightly stale country-style bread
750g (1½lb) very ripe tomatoes
¼ tsp dried oregano
salt
best quality extra-virgin olive oil

PREPARATION

1 Preheat the oven to 150°C/300°F/gas 2.
2 Lay the slices of bread on a baking tray and bake for 15 minutes – the bread should become dry and crisp but not coloured.
3 Break the toasted bread into chunks and briefly dampen it under running water, being careful not to soak it. Squeeze it dry with your hands.
4 Place the bread in the bottom of a serving bowl. Provided the tomatoes are sufficiently ripe, you should be able to squeeze them over the bread, so that the juice and flesh come out, leaving the skin which should be discarded. Alternatively, skin and chop the tomatoes and scatter over the bread.
5 Sprinkle the salad with oregano and a generous helping of salt. Drizzle with olive oil and leave to stand for 20 minutes before serving.

VARIATION

• Add extra ingredients such as chopped red onion, cucumber, mozzarella, olives or anchovies. Use fresh oregano, basil or parsley instead of dried oregano.

FATTOUSH

Lebanese bread salad

This salad has a base of flat bread soaked in vegetable juices and a lemony dressing that makes it substantial and refreshing. As with many eastern Mediterranean salads, plenty of herbs are used. If you can find purslane in the summer, do include it for an authentic flavour — it is easily recognizable by its fleshy stalks.

INGREDIENTS

½ cucumber
1 bunch spring onions
500g (1 lb) ripe tomatoes, skinned and chopped
salt
1 large flat bread or 2 pitta breads
1 cos lettuce heart
1 large bunch fresh parsley
1 large bunch fresh mint
1 large bunch purslane, optional
150ml (¼ pint) extra-virgin olive oil
125ml (4fl oz) fresh lemon juice
black pepper

PREPARATION

1 Peel the cucumber and dice the flesh. Chop the spring onions, including the green tops, into fine rounds and mix with the tomatoes and cucumber. Sprinkle with salt and leave to stand for 10 minutes.
2 Toast the bread until lightly browned. Break it into 2.5cm (1in) squares and scatter them over the base of a serving dish. Cover with the tomato, cucumber and spring onion mix, making sure you pour in all the juices. Leave to stand for a further 10 minutes for the bread to absorb the juices.
3 Roughly chop the lettuce, parsley and mint, discarding large stalks. Strip the purslane leaves from the stalk, if using. Mix the herbs into the salad.
4 Whisk together the oil and lemon juice until the mixture emulsifies, then season with pepper. Pour this dressing over the salad and serve.

PIZZA ALLA MARINARA

Pizza with tomato sauce

The Neapolitans, who invented the dish, say that pizzas must be cooked in a wood-fired oven. This method may produce an incomparable flavour, but home-cooked pizzas can still be good. This is the original version, with a simple tomato sauce. Makes 2 large pizzas.

INGREDIENTS

PIZZA DOUGH
1 tsp sugar
15g (½oz) dried yeast
½ tsp salt
45ml (3 tbsps) olive oil, plus oil for sprinkling
625g (1¼lb) strong plain flour, plus flour to dust
TOMATO SAUCE
60ml (4 tbsps) olive oil, plus oil for greasing
4 cloves garlic, finely chopped
1kg (2lb) very ripe plum tomatoes, skinned, deseeded and chopped
salt
2 tsps dried oregano
black pepper

PREPARATION

1 Beat the sugar into 300ml (½ pint) warm water until it dissolves. Whisk in the yeast. Cover with clingfilm and leave for 15 minutes, until frothy.
2 Stir the salt and olive oil into the yeast mixture. Pour the flour onto a board and make a well in its centre. Gradually add the yeast mixture, working with your hands to incorporate it. When all the liquid has been absorbed, work the dough until it is smooth and pliable (see page 151).
3 Place the dough in a lightly floured bowl and sprinkle a little oil over the surface. Cover with a clean tea towel and leave in a warm place for 1 hour, or until doubled in volume.
4 Make the tomato sauce. Heat 45ml (3 tbsps) of oil and add the garlic. As soon as it starts to sizzle, add the tomatoes. Simmer, uncovered, for 15–20 minutes, stirring frequently. The sauce should be thick and garlicky. Add salt to taste.
5 Preheat the oven to maximum. Knock back the dough (see page 151) and divide it in half. Oil a baking sheet and thinly spread half the dough across it with your hands, leaving the edges slightly thicker.
6 Spread the base with half the sauce, sprinkle with half the oregano and plenty of pepper, then drizzle over 15ml (1 tbsp) of olive oil. Repeat with the remaining dough and sauce.
7 Bake at the top of the oven for 12–15 minutes, until the edges of the pizza are crisp. Eat very hot.

COCA MALLORQUINA

Majorcan-style pizza

Perhaps more like the Pissaladière (see page 48) than the Italian pizza, a coca is a slowly cooked bread-based tart. Ham or sausage can be added to the vegetable topping.

INGREDIENTS

DOUGH

1 tsp sugar
15g (½oz) dried yeast
300g (10oz) strong plain flour
½ tsp salt
30g (1oz) lard, diced
15ml (1 tbsp) olive oil

TOPPING

3 small white onions
3 green peppers, cored, deseeded and thinly sliced
2 large tomatoes, thinly sliced
3 cloves garlic, finely chopped
2 tbsps chopped fresh parsley
2 tsps sweet paprika
salt and black pepper
60ml (4 tbsps) olive oil

PREPARATION

1 Mix the sugar with 150ml (¼ pint) warm water, then beat in the yeast. Cover with clingfilm and leave in a warm place for 15 minutes, until frothy.
2 Sift the flour with the salt in a mixing bowl. Crumble the lard into the flour. Add the oil and rub it into the flour with the lard.
3 Make a well in the centre of the flour mixture and pour in the yeast solution. Mix quickly with your hands, until you have a smooth pliable dough (see page 151). Knead briefly then place in a bowl, cover with a clean tea towel and leave in a warm place for 1 hour, or until doubled in volume.
4 Meanwhile, peel the onions, cut in half and slice into fine half-moons. Mix them with the peppers, tomatoes, garlic, parsley and paprika. Season well.
5 Knock back the dough (see page 151) and knead again. Preheat the oven to 180°C/350°F/gas 4.
6 Stretch out the dough to fill a 30cm (12in) baking tin, making a slightly raised edge. Pile on the vegetable topping then pour over the oil.
7 Bake for 1 hour, until the vegetables are soft and lightly browned on top and the rim of the coca is crisp. Serve warm, not piping hot.

PASTA CON LE SARDE
Pasta with sardines

This ancient Sicilian dish gets its unusual flavour from the wild fennel stalks that flavour the water in which the pasta is cooked. If you can't find wild fennel, substitute the stalks and feathery fronds of cultivated fennel and a little of the bulb.

INGREDIENTS

250g (8oz) fennel stalks
salt
1 large onion, chopped
90g (3oz) sultanas
90g (3oz) pine kernels
¼ tsp saffron
150ml (¼ pint) olive oil
black pepper
6 fresh sardines
375–500g (12oz–1lb) bucatini
4 anchovy fillets
¼ lemon

PREPARATION

1 Wash the fennel well. Put 4 litres (7 pints) of water in a large pot and add a teaspoon of salt. Bring to the boil, add the fennel stalks and then simmer for 10 minutes.
2 Put the onion in a heavy pan together with 400ml (14fl oz) of water. Bring to the boil and simmer uncovered for 10 minutes. Meanwhile, soak the sultanas in warm water for 10 minutes.
3 Drain the fennel well, reserving the cooking water, and chop it finely. Add the fennel, drained sultanas, pine kernels, saffron, three-quarters of the oil and plenty of pepper to the pan with the onion. Cover and leave to cook for 15 minutes.
4 Cut off the heads and tails of the sardines and gut the fish (see page 152). Carefully remove the backbone and pick out any remaining stray bones (don't worry if the fillets fall apart).
5 Bring the water in which the fennel was cooked back to the boil and add the bucatini. Cook for 10–12 minutes, until *al dente* (see page 156).
6 Meanwhile, add the sardine fillets to the sauce and cook for 5 minutes. In a separate frying pan, heat the remaining oil and add the anchovies. Fry gently for 3–4 minutes, stirring continuously with a wooden spoon, until the anchovies have broken down, then add the contents of the pan to the sauce.
7 Drain the pasta, reserving 2 tablespoons of its cooking liquid. Add this to the sauce and then quickly toss the pasta in it.
8 Finish the dish with a squeeze of lemon and serve immediately.

PASTA E FAGIOLI
Pasta and beans

Technically a soup, this rustic dish is sufficiently substantial and nutritious to be a main meal in itself. It is popular throughout Italy – I have enjoyed especially fine versions in Tuscany, when fresh borlotti beans were in season, and in Naples, where all sorts of odds and ends of pasta had found their way into the dish.

INGREDIENTS

250g (8oz) dried cannellini or borlotti beans, soaked overnight or 2 x 425g (14oz) cans cooked beans, drained or 750g (1½lb) fresh beans
45ml (3 tbsps) olive oil
2 sticks celery, including leaves, chopped
90g (3oz) Parma ham trimmings or pancetta, chopped
2 fat cloves garlic, chopped
2 small dried red chillies, finely chopped
1 large sprig fresh rosemary
1 tbsp tomato purée
3 plum tomatoes, skinned and deseeded
1.25 litres (2 pints) chicken or vegetable stock (see page 155)
salt and black pepper
125g (4oz) dried pasta, such as maltagliati or spaghetti broken up into short lengths
extra-virgin olive oil and freshly grated Parmesan, to serve

PREPARATION

1 Simmer the dried beans in plenty of unsalted water for 2 hours or until soft (fresh beans take 30 minutes; canned beans need only to be rinsed).
2 Heat the oil in a heavy pan and add the celery and Parma ham. Cook over a gentle heat for 5 minutes. Add the garlic, chillies and rosemary and cook for a further 5 minutes.
3 Dissolve the tomato purée in a little warm water. Add to the pan with the tomatoes and cook for a further 10 minutes, stirring occasionally.
4 Drain the beans and add two-thirds of them to the pan together with the stock and seasoning. Bring to the boil and add the pasta. Cook, uncovered, for 10 minutes, until the pasta is tender.
5 Purée the remaining beans in a food processor. When the pasta is cooked, stir this purée into the soup to thicken it.
6 Serve the soup, offering around small bowls of extra-virgin olive oil and Parmesan for each diner to help themselves.

VARIATIONS

• Use chick-peas instead of beans.
• Omit the rosemary and add a handful of torn basil leaves at the last minute.

ORECCHIETTE AL RAGU

Little ears with tomato sauce and meatballs

Orecchiette, or "little ears", are the favourite pasta of the southern Italian region of Apulia and in particular its capital, the seaport of Bari. Served with ragù, a slowly cooked tomato sauce, and meatballs, this pasta makes an excellent winter dish. Traditionally, the pork belly is reserved and served as a separate main course.

INGREDIENTS

45ml (3 tbsps) olive oil
1 large onion, chopped
250g (8oz) pork belly, in one piece
3 cloves garlic, finely chopped
250ml (8fl oz) red wine
750g (1½lb) plum tomatoes, skinned, deseeded and chopped
400g (13oz) can whole peeled tomatoes, chopped
1 tbsp tomato purée
bouquet garni made up of 1 fresh bay leaf and 3 sprigs each of fresh oregano, rosemary and thyme
salt and black pepper
500g (1lb) minced beef
60g (2oz) finely grated Parmesan, plus Parmesan to serve
30g (1oz) fresh white breadcrumbs
4 tbsps finely chopped fresh parsley
375–500g (12oz–1lb) orecchiette

PREPARATION

1 Ragù is best cooked in an earthenware pot. Heat the oil and add the onion and the piece of pork belly. Cook over a moderate heat for 20 minutes, stirring frequently, until both the meat and the onion are browned. Add two-thirds of the garlic and cook for a further 5 minutes.

2 Turn up the heat and pour in the red wine. Allow to bubble fiercely for 5 minutes before adding both the fresh and canned tomatoes and tomato purée.

3 Turn the heat down as low as possible, add the bouquet garni and seasoning to taste, cover and leave to cook for 2–3 hours, stirring occasionally. The slower the sauce cooks, the better it will taste.

4 Meanwhile mix together the minced beef, Parmesan, breadcrumbs, parsley and remaining garlic. Preheat the grill. Mould the mixture into walnut-sized balls and grill for 10 minutes, turning them halfway through, until browned all over.

5 Add the meatballs to the tomato sauce, which should be very thick, and cook for 30 minutes.

6 Bring some salted water to the boil, add the orecchiette and cook until *al dente* (see page 156).

7 Remove the pork belly from the tomato sauce. Check the seasoning, pour the sauce over the drained pasta and serve with plenty of Parmesan.

Tomatoes

Red wine

Garlic

Onion

Olive oil

Pork belly

Canned
tomatoes

Tomato
purée

Bouquet garni

Salt

Black
pepper

Minced
beef

Parmesan

Breadcrumbs

Parsley

Orecchiette

SPAGHETTI ALLA PUTTANESCA

Spaghetti with spicy sauce

This is known as the whores' spaghetti, though I can't imagine their business would be very good after they had eaten this garlic-laden dish. My own theory is that because it uses storecupboard goods they were able to prepare it at the end of the night's work, before the shops opened.

INGREDIENTS

60g (2oz) anchovy fillets in olive oil
60ml (4 tbsps) olive oil
4 cloves garlic, finely chopped
1 small dried chilli, finely chopped
2 x 400g (13oz) can whole peeled tomatoes, chopped in the can
1 tsp dried oregano
black pepper
125g (4oz) black olives
375–500g (12oz–1lb) spaghetti
2 tbsps capers, rinsed and drained
salt

PREPARATION

1 Drain the anchovies from the oil and chop their flesh coarsely. Heat the olive oil over a low heat and add the anchovies. Cook, stirring all the time, until the anchovies have dissolved into the oil.
2 Turn up the heat and add the garlic and chilli. As soon as the garlic begins to sizzle, add the tomatoes, oregano and plenty of pepper. Bring the sauce to the boil, stirring continuously to help break up the tomatoes. Reduce to a gentle simmer and cook for 30 minutes, stirring from time to time, until the tomatoes have broken down and made a thick sauce.
3 Meanwhile slice the flesh from around the stones of the olives. Bring a large pan of heavily salted water to the boil.
4 Add the spaghetti to the water and the capers and olives to the tomato sauce. When the spaghetti is *al dente* (see page 156), drain it, reserving a tablespoon of the cooking water.
5 Taste the sauce, adding salt if necessary. Toss the pasta with the reserved cooking water and then with the sauce.

CANALONS

Stuffed baked pasta

It is not just the Italians who enjoy pasta – this stuffed pasta dish is a speciality of Barcelona. On Fridays the canalons are stuffed with spinach and salt cod, but the rest of the week a rich mixture of pork and chicken livers is the favourite. Illustrated on page 128.

INGREDIENTS

45ml (3 tbsps) olive oil
1 onion, finely chopped
2 cloves garlic, finely chopped
250g (8oz) plum tomatoes, skinned, deseeded and chopped
375g (12oz) finely minced pork
175g (6oz) chicken livers, finely chopped
salt and black pepper
2 pinches nutmeg
1 large egg, beaten
30g (1oz) fresh white breadcrumbs
16 canoli pasta wrappers or 12 cannelloni tubes
90g (3oz) butter, plus butter to grease
60g (2oz) plain flour
600ml (1 pint) full-cream milk
90g (3oz) freshly grated Parmesan

PREPARATION

1 Heat the oil in a heavy frying pan over a medium heat. When the oil is hot, add the onion, reduce the heat and cook for 25 minutes, stirring occasionally, until the onion is golden and slightly caramelized.
2 Add the garlic and cook for a further 5 minutes, then add the tomatoes. Cook for a further 10 minutes, still stirring regularly, until the tomatoes have completely broken down. You now have the *sofregit* (see page 156) that is the basis of so much Catalan cooking.
3 Turn up the heat to medium and add the pork and chicken livers, together with the seasoning and nutmeg. Cook for 10 minutes, stirring regularly to break up the meat, until the pork and liver mixture is evenly cooked. Take off the heat and stir in the egg and breadcrumbs.
4 Bring a large pan of salted water to the boil and cook the canoli wrappers for 3 minutes or the cannelloni tubes for 4 minutes. Drain and refresh under cold water. Separate and lay on a plate.
5 Now make a roux by melting the butter and stirring in the flour. Cook over a low heat for 3–4 minutes, stirring continuously with a wooden spoon, until the roux is light brown.
6 Meanwhile warm the milk until hot. Slowly pour the milk into the roux, stirring all the time, until you have a smooth sauce. Allow to bubble for 3 minutes, still stirring.

7 Preheat the oven to 180°C/350°F/gas 4.

8 Grease an earthenware dish with butter. Lay a little of the meat mixture along one side of each of the canoli wrappers and roll up, placing them join-side down in the dish. Alternatively, push some filling into each of the cannelloni tubes.

9 Pour over sufficient white sauce to cover the canoli. Sprinkle the Parmesan over the top. Bake in the preheated oven for 45 minutes, until the surface is nicely browned and the sauce bubbling.

RISOTTO DI CARCIOFI

Artichoke risotto

In the early months of the year, tiny purple artichokes arrive in the Venetian markets. This risotto is a favourite way of serving them, and also works well with larger globe artichokes.

INGREDIENTS

4 globe artichokes
90g (3oz) butter
30ml (2 tbsps) olive oil
1 small onion or 4 shallots, finely chopped
1.25 litres (2 pints) light chicken stock (see page 155)
300g (10oz) arborio rice
salt and black pepper
60g (2oz) freshly grated Parmesan

PREPARATION

1 Prepare the artichokes (see page 150), then cut the hearts into very thin strips.

2 Heat three-quarters of the butter with the oil in a large heavy pan. Gently sweat the onion for 10 minutes, until soft.

3 Warm the chicken stock to simmering point in a separate pan.

4 Add the shreds of artichoke and the rice to the onion, stirring well to coat with the fat and adding plenty of seasoning. When the rice is thoroughly coated, pour over 1 ladleful of the simmering stock. Cook over a medium heat, until all the liquid is absorbed.

5 Continue to add the hot stock, a ladleful at a time, until the rice is plump and tender but still firm to the bite. This will take 20–25 minutes – taste to check. Adjust the seasoning, then stir in the remaining butter and Parmesan and serve.

VARIATION

• Replace the artichokes with 250g (8oz) of wild mushrooms (ceps and horns of plenty are especially good), cleaned and sliced thinly.

MEJADARRA

Rice with lentils and onions

This Lebanese dish uses simple ingredients to great effect. The key to its success is the crispy onion fried in olive oil that tops the rice and lentils. Served with chilled natural yogurt, it makes a very satisfying vegetarian main meal. Serves 4 as a main dish or 6 as a side dish.

INGREDIENTS

250g (8oz) long-grain rice
250g (8oz) brown lentils
5 large onions
150ml (¼ pint) olive oil
1 tsp ground cumin
1 tsp ground coriander
½ tsp sweet paprika
salt and black pepper

PREPARATION

1 Soak the rice for at least an hour in plenty of water. Pick over the lentils to remove any impurities and rinse thoroughly under cold running water. Peel the onions, chop 2 of them very finely and cut the remaining 3 in half and slice into fine half-moons.

2 Bring a large pan of water to the boil and boil the lentils hard for 10 minutes. Fry the finely chopped onions in 30ml (2 tbsps) of oil, stirring frequently, until lightly browned all over.

3 Drain the lentils and mix in the fried onion, spices and plenty of seasoning. Add 1.5 litres (2½ pints) of cold water, bring to the boil and allow to boil uncovered for 10-15 minutes, until the lentils are cooked through but not disintegrating.

4 Drain and rinse the rice, and add to the pot. Boil uncovered for 5 minutes, until most of the liquid has been absorbed. Turn the heat down as low as it will go, cover, and leave for 20 minutes.

5 Meanwhile, warm the remaining oil in a frying pan over a medium-high heat. When it is very hot, add the onion slices and fry for 15–20 minutes, stirring frequently, until brown and caramelized.

6 Put the rice and lentil mixture in a large bowl, scatter with the crispy fried onions and pour over the oil from the pan. Leave to stand for 10 minutes before serving. The dish is also good served cold.

CANALONS
Stuffed baked pasta
(page 126)

IÇ PILAVI
Pilav with chicken livers
(page 130)

COUSCOUS AUX SEPT LEGUMES
Couscous with seven vegetables
(page 131)

IÇ PILAVI

Pilav with chicken livers

This rich dish is of Ottoman heritage. Turkish pilavs are typically served as accompaniments to grilled meats, but this dish with chicken livers is usually served on its own. Illustrated on page 128.

INGREDIENTS

250g (8oz) long-grain rice
90g (3oz) butter
15ml (1 tbsp) olive oil
1 onion, finely chopped
1 tbsp pine kernels
2 tbsps flaked almonds
250g (8oz) chicken livers, finely chopped
2 tbsps currants
1 tsp sweet paprika
salt and black pepper
2 tsps finely chopped fresh parsley

PREPARATION

1 Soak the rice in plenty of water for at least 1 hour. Drain and rinse under cold water.
2 Melt half the butter with the oil in a large heavy frying pan with a lid over a low heat. Add the onion and sweat gently for 10 minutes, until soft.
3 Turn up the heat and add the pine kernels, almonds and chicken livers. Fry for 5 minutes, stirring constantly, until the nuts are lightly browned and the chicken livers cooked through.
4 Melt the remaining butter in a large pan and add the rice, currants and paprika. Cook gently for 3 minutes, stirring continuously to coat the rice grains in the oil.
5 Bring 600ml (1 pint) of water to the boil, pour over the rice, season, stir once and cover. Simmer gently for 12 minutes, until the water is absorbed.
6 Take the rice off the heat and stir in the chicken liver and nut mixture. Cover with a tea towel and replace the lid. Leave for 10 minutes then fluff the rice with a fork, sprinkle with parsley and serve.

ROZ BI SAFFRAN

Morrocan rice with dried fruit and nuts

Illustrated on page 47.

INGREDIENTS

375g (12oz) long-grain rice
60g (2oz) butter
¼ tsp saffron
½ tsp salt
125–150g (4–5oz) mixed pine kernels, hazelnuts, dried apricots and raisins

PREPARATION

1 Soak the rice in plenty of water for at least 1 hour. Drain, rinse under cold water and spread on a tray to dry for 30 minutes.
2 Melt three-quarters of the butter in a large heavy pan with a lid. Stir in the rice and saffron.
3 Pour over 900ml (1½ pints) of water, add salt and bring rapidly to the boil. Boil for 2 minutes, turn the heat right down and cover the pan. Leave to cook for 20 minutes, until the liquid is absorbed.
4 Take the rice off the heat and cover with a dry tea towel. Leave to stand for 10 minutes.
5 Melt the remaining butter and toss the pine kernels and hazelnuts in it for 1 minute, until lightly browned. Add the dried fruit and cook for a further minute, until warm. Stir into the rice.

TABBOULEH

Cracked wheat and herb salad

This Lebanese salad is traditionally served with crisp lettuce leaves to scoop up the herby, lemon-sharp mixture.

INGREDIENTS

175g (6oz) fine bulgur wheat, soaked for 20–25 minutes
8 spring onions, green tops removed
3 tomatoes, skinned
1 large bunch fresh parsley, stalks removed
1 small bunch fresh mint, stalks removed
juice of 2–3 lemons
175ml (6fl oz) olive oil
salt and black pepper

PREPARATION

1 Drain the bulgur wheat and squeeze dry with your hands. Finely chop the spring onions, tomatoes and herbs, then mix with the bulgur wheat.
2 Beat together the lemon juice and olive oil until emulsified, and season. Pour over the salad, adding more lemon juice if desired. Leave for 30 minutes, until the grains are tender. Serve with crisp lettuce.

COUSCOUS AUX SEPT LEGUMES

Couscous with seven vegetables·

The key to couscous is not the fine semolina grain itself, but the luxuriant sauce with which it is served. This version from the magical Moroccan city of Fez brings together the produce of the vegetable market in a delicately spiced broth. You can use whatever vegetables are available, but there must always be seven for luck. Serves 6–8. Illustrated on page 129.

INGREDIENTS

175g (6oz) dried chick-peas, soaked overnight
2 lamb bones, optional
2 chicken wings, optional
3 cloves garlic, chopped
1 cinnamon stick
½ tsp saffron
½ tsp turmeric
1 tsp black pepper
90g (3oz) butter
1 bunch each fresh coriander and parsley
2 onions, grated
500g (1lb) plum tomatoes, skinned and chopped
500g (1lb) carrots, peeled
500g (1lb) small turnips, peeled
250g (8oz) raisins
1 tsp salt
500g (1lb) pumpkin
500g (1lb) courgettes
250g (8oz) shelled broad beans and fresh peas
500g (1lb) quick-cook couscous
harissa, to serve (see page 30)

PREPARATION

1 Place the chick-peas in a large pan or couscousier with the lamb bones and chicken wings (if using), garlic, spices, half the butter, three-quarters of the herbs tied in a bunch, the onion and tomatoes. Pour over 3.5 litres (5¾ pints) of water.
2 Bring to the boil, then reduce the heat and simmer the mixture, covered, for 1½ hours, until the chick-peas are tender.
3 Cut the carrots across at 2.5cm (1in) intervals. Halve or quarter any larger turnips, leaving the very small ones whole. Remove any bones, chicken wings and herbs from the stock and discard. Add the carrots, turnips, raisins and the salt and continue to simmer.
4 Peel the pumpkin and cut into 5cm (2in) chunks. Cut the courgettes in half lengthways and then in half across. Twenty minutes after adding the first group of vegetables, add the remaining ones. Simmer for a further 20 minutes.

5 Meanwhile, steam the couscous according to the instructions on the packet (if you are using a couscousier you can do this over the broth). Pile the hot couscous onto a large serving dish and dot with the remaining butter.
6 Check the seasoning of the broth, adding more salt if necessary. Finely chop the remaining herbs and add them to the pan. Serve the broth in a large tureen, allowing each diner to help themselves. There should also be a small pot of harissa paste on the table.

COUSCOUS AL SAMAK

Fish couscous

The Moroccans are not the only eaters of couscous – this is the classic Tunisian version. You will also find fish couscous on the western edge of Sicily, particularly in Trapani. It is a legacy of the island's Arab occupation more than a thousand years ago. Serves 6–8.

INGREDIENTS

125g (4oz) chick-peas, soaked overnight
1.5 kg (3lb) mixed fish, such as red mullet,
grey mullet, sea bream, sea bass, scaled and gutted
(see page 152)
3 large carrots, thickly sliced
3 onions, quartered
3 small turnips, peeled and quartered
4 large plum tomatoes, quartered
¼ tsp saffron
¼–½ tsp cayenne pepper
salt and black pepper
500g (1lb) quick-cook couscous
butter, to serve

PREPARATION

1 Place the chick-peas in a pan or couscousier with 2 litres (3½ pints) of water. Bring to the boil, then reduce the heat and simmer for 30 minutes. Meanwhile, remove the heads and tails of the fish. Add these trimmings to the pot and cook for a further 30 minutes.
2 Remove the fish heads and tails from the pot and add the vegetables, saffron, cayenne and plenty of seasoning. Leave to simmer uncovered for a further hour, until the vegetables are very tender.
3 Cut the fish into thick slices and add to the broth. Simmer for 10–15 minutes, until cooked through.
4 Steam the couscous according to the instructions on the packet (if you are using a couscousier you can do this over the broth). Pile the hot couscous onto a large serving dish and dot with butter. Serve with the hot fish broth.

PRESERVES

Today most foodstuffs are continuously available, but the tradition of preserving, bottling and pickling remains in the Mediterranean and many of the products of these ancient culinary arts have become delicacies in their own right. Preserved artichoke hearts and sweet red peppers, for example, make simple but stunning antipasti, fruit bottled in sweet mustard oil, *mostardi di frutti*, are a celebrated Italian speciality, while bottled or crystallized fruits make delectable, fragrant sweetmeats popular throughout the region.

CANDIED PUMPKIN

Crystallized pumpkin is very popular in the eastern Mediterranean, especially Turkey. It can be used in baking but is also a delicious sweetmeat. Use small pumpkins.

INGREDIENTS

1kg (2lb) slice of pumpkin
250g (8oz) white sugar

PREPARATION

1 Remove the rind and seeds of the pumpkin. Cut the flesh into 1cm (½in) thick finger-length strips.
2 Place the sugar in a large wide pan with 150ml (¼ pint) of water. Bring slowly to the boil, stirring continuously so that the sugar dissolves.
3 Arrange the pumpkin strips in a single layer. Simmer gently in the syrup for 45 minutes, stirring regularly to prevent the strips of pumpkin from sticking together. The pumpkin should be very soft and translucent.
4 Arrange the strips of pumpkin on greaseproof paper on a baking tray, making sure the strips are not touching each other. Put the oven to its lowest setting. Leave the pumpkin slices in the oven overnight or for 10–12 hours.
5 Remove from the oven and allow to cool – the pumpkin will become crisp. It will keep in an airtight container for up to 3 months.

VARIATION

• Instead of drying the slices of pumpkin in the oven, allow them to cool in the syrup, to which you have added 2 teaspoons of rose-water. Serve in very small quantities with clotted or rich cream and walnuts.

CONSERVA DI PEPERONI

Preserved peppers

Although peppers are now available all year round, they are still worth preserving. Peppers kept in this way develop a concentrated sweetness, making them ideal as a little antipasto, served with a few marinated olives and a slice of good bread.

INGREDIENTS

1kg (2lb) red peppers
2 tbsps coarse sea salt
handful of fresh basil leaves

PREPARATION

1 Grill the peppers until the skins are blackened and then peel them (see page 150).
2 Rinse the peeled peppers thoroughly under cold water. Cut the flesh into strips.
3 Pack the peppers into a sterilized lidded preserving jar in which they just fit, layering with the salt and basil leaves.
4 Place the jar in a pan, cover it with cold water, bring to the boil and boil for 15 minutes. The peppers will keep for up to 6 months.

VARIATION

• The Italians preserve peppers in white wine vinegar – *peperoni sott' aceto*. Pour a bottle of good quality wine vinegar into a pan and bring to the boil. Add 4–6 cored, sliced red peppers and simmer for 15 minutes. Season with salt and pour into a sterilized preserving jar. Tuck in a few fresh bay leaves and leave for 2 months before using.

DULCE DE MEMBRILLO

Quince paste

*This thick orange-coloured paste, heavy with the
perfume of quinces, is often served in Spain with a slice
of Manchego cheese as a snack or to end a meal.*

INGREDIENTS

*2kg (4lb) quinces
white sugar
butter, to grease baking tray*

PREPARATION

1 Peel and core the quinces. Roughly chop the
flesh and put it in a heavy pan with 125ml (4fl oz)
of water. Bring the water to the boil, turn down to
a simmer, cover and leave to cook for 30 minutes.
2 At the end of this time you will have a purée.
Push it through a sieve to remove lumps.
3 Weigh the purée and stir in 275g (9oz) of sugar
per 500g (1lb) of pulp. Return it to the pan and
simmer for 45 minutes, uncovered.
4 Pour the mixture into a lightly greased oblong
baking tray, to the depth of about 2.5cm (1in). Let
cool and cut into squares. It will keep for 1 month
stored in a tin or wrapped in greaseproof paper.

MARINATED OLIVES

*Shop-bought olives in brine can sometimes seem a little
dull. In order to improve their flavour, bottle them in
oil infused with fragrant herbs and garlic, or perhaps add
some small dried red chillies and orange zest.*

INGREDIENTS

*500g (1lb) mixed black and green olives
2 cloves garlic, peeled
1 sprig fresh thyme
1 sprig fresh rosemary
1 fresh bay leaf
1 piece lemon zest
450ml (¾ pint) extra-virgin olive oil, to cover*

PREPARATION

1 Rinse the olives well then pack them in a
preserving jar together with the garlic, herbs and
lemon zest. Pour in sufficient olive oil to cover.
2 Leave for 2–3 weeks for the flavours
to develop. Olives keep for up to 6 months.

PRESERVED LEMONS

*The sharpness of lemon juice plays a key part
in Mediterranean cookery. It is difficult to imagine this
region without its groves of citrus fruit trees,
but the lemon and orange were first introduced to the
area by the Romans who brought seedlings from India.
The Moors revitalized their popularity, planting groves in
Sicily and southern Spain. Today the Moroccans preserve
lemons in salt for use in fragrant tagines.*

INGREDIENTS

*6 unwaxed lemons
125g (4oz) coarse sea salt
1 fresh bay leaf
2 cloves
6 coriander seeds
6 black peppercorns
freshly squeezed lemon juice, to cover*

PREPARATION

1 Soak the lemons in water for 2 days, changing
the water once.
2 Quarter the lemons from the top to within 1cm
(½in) of the bottom. Sprinkle plenty of salt onto
the cut flesh, then reshape the lemons.
3 Place half the remaining salt on the base of a
sterilized preserving jar, then pack in the lemons,
bay leaf and spices. Add the remaining salt and
press down on the lemons to release their juices.
4 Cover with lemon juice and leave for at least
1 month (they will keep for up to 6 months).
5 Rinse the lemons well before use.

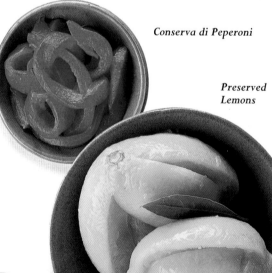

Conserva di Peperoni

*Preserved
Lemons*

DESSERTS

Sweet dishes are typically eaten separately in the Mediterranean, rather than at the end of the meal. Sticky pastries, laden with honey, are usually enjoyed with a cup of coffee in a specialist bakery; ice-creams are eaten at the *gelateria* or the *heladeria*. The meal itself often ends with a simple bowl of fruit, or a pudding made from those fruits. What could be nicer and more refreshing than wild strawberries served in a chilled glass of red wine, figs baked with scented honey or peaches stuffed with almond paste?

SIKA STO FOURNO
Baked figs

A fresh fig is one of the greatest treats that the Mediterranean region has to offer — especially if it is eaten almost as soon as it is picked from the tree on which it has ripened to perfection. In Greece, slightly under-ripe figs are baked with a little scented honey from the sacred mount of Hymettus to bring out their full flavour.

INGREDIENTS
8 figs
juice of 1 orange
125ml (4fl oz) Samos or other sweet wine
2 tbsps clear honey, preferably Hymettus honey
30ml (2 tbsps) orange-flower water, optional
Greek natural yogurt, to serve

PREPARATION
1 Preheat the oven to 150°C/300°F/gas 2.
2 Make deep crosses in the top of the figs and place them in a gratin dish in which they just fit.
3 Gently heat together the orange juice, wine and honey and pour this over the figs, making sure plenty gets down into the cracks.
4 Bake the figs in the preheated oven for 40 minutes, spooning over the juices several times, until the figs are very soft. Sprinkle over the orange-flower water and serve immediately with creamy natural yogurt.

VARIATION
• Serve the figs with fresh cream slightly sweetened with caster sugar and infused with a few strands of saffron soaked in a little warm water.

PERAS ESTOFADOS
Poached pears

This is a beautiful dish — the poached pears burnished gold with honey and dark Oloroso sherry sit in a pool of syrup redolent with cinnamon and saffron.

INGREDIENTS
8 slightly under-ripe pears
juice and grated zest of 1 lemon
250g (8oz) honey
175ml (6fl oz) Oloroso sherry
2 cloves
1 stick cinnamon
good pinch of saffron
8 blanched almonds, optional

PREPARATION
1 Peel the pears and pack them stalk upwards in a heavy pan. Pour over the lemon juice.
2 Mix together the remaining ingredients with 600ml (1 pint) of water and boil for 5–10 minutes, until you have a syrup. Pour this mixture over the pears, bring back to the boil and then turn down to a bare simmer. Poach the pears gently for 20 minutes, leaving the pan uncovered.
3 Discard the cinnamon stick and cloves. Remove the pears and reduce the syrup by fast boiling for 5 minutes. Return the pears to the liquid and leave to cool. Before serving, replace the stalks of the pears with the whole almonds, if desired.

PESCHE RIPIENE

Stuffed peaches

A perfect peach should be enjoyed just as it is. But even in Italy not all peaches are perfect, so under-ripe ones are stuffed with a macaroon mixture and baked in white wine.

INGREDIENTS

4 peaches
2 macaroons
8 blanched almonds
1 egg yolk
45g (1½oz) caster sugar
1 tsp grated lemon zest
butter, to coat dish
100ml (3½fl oz) sweet white wine
flaked almonds, optional

PREPARATION

1 Halve the peaches and remove the stone. Scoop out a little of the flesh to make a deeper hole.
2 Put the macaroons, almonds, egg yolk, two-thirds of the sugar, the lemon zest and the scooped out peach flesh in a food processor and work until you have a smooth paste. Stuff the hollows in the peaches with this mixture.
3 Preheat the oven to 160°C/325°F/gas 3. Lightly butter an earthenware ovenproof dish and arrange the stuffed peaches in it. Pour over the wine and sprinkle the peaches with the remaining sugar. Bake for 30 minutes.
4 Meanwhile, toast the flaked almonds under a hot grill. Remove the peaches from the oven and leave them to cool in the liquid. Serve warm or at room temperature, sprinkled with almonds.

FRAISES DE BOIS AU VIN ROUGE

Provençal wild strawberries in red wine

In the western Mediterranean, dessert is often fruit marinated in wine or spirits – perhaps peaches or nectarines in Sauternes, bilberries with grappa or this favourite of mine, tiny woodland strawberries in chilled red wine.

INGREDIENTS

500g (1lb) wild or small strawberries, rinsed and dried
2 tbsps caster sugar
2 glasses Beaujolais or other light, fruity red wine
4 fresh mint leaves

PREPARATION

1 Sprinkle the strawberries with sugar and place them in 4 tall wine glasses.
2 Pour in sufficient Beaujolais to cover the berries. Decorate with a mint leaf and chill thoroughly.

KHOSHAF

Dried fruit and nut salad

This Lebanese favourite is made distinctive by the perfumed marinade that infuses the dried fruit.

INGREDIENTS

375g (12oz) dried apricots
175g (6oz) seedless raisins
125g (4oz) caster sugar
15ml (1 tbsp) rose-water
15ml (1 tbsp) orange-flower water
175g (6oz) blanched almonds or a mixture of almonds and pistachio nuts

PREPARATION

1 Place the dried fruits in a large bowl and sprinkle over the sugar and the scented waters.
2 Pour in just enough cold water to cover the fruits and leave in a warm place for 48 hours.
3 Add the nuts and chill well before serving.

TARTE AU CITRON

Lemon tart

Though lemon tart is now popular throughout France, especially in the brasseries of Paris, it is only in the south that the lemon trees grow. To make sure you capture the elusive fragrance of the lemon, do use unwaxed fruit.

INGREDIENTS

250g (8oz) plain flour
pinch of salt
200g (7oz) caster sugar
125g (4oz) unsalted butter
1 egg yolk, plus 5 eggs, separated
60ml (4 tbsps) iced water
zest and juice of 3 lemons, preferably unwaxed
1 tsp cornflour

PREPARATION

1 Sift the flour with the salt and 90g (3oz) of sugar. Cut the butter into small cubes and crumble it into the flour with your fingers.
2 Make a well in the centre of the butter and flour mixture and add the egg yolk and the iced water. Stir well until you have a smooth paste. Wrap in clingfilm and chill for 1 hour.
3 Beat the remaining egg yolks with 90g (3oz) of sugar until light and creamy. Add the zest and juice of the lemons and then carefully stir in the cornflour, ensuring there are no lumps. Pour into a heavy-based pan and heat gently for 5 minutes, stirring constantly, until the mixture thickens – do not allow the mixture to boil or it will curdle.
4 Preheat the oven to 180°C/350°F/gas 4. Roll out the pastry thinly and line a buttered 25cm (10in) tart tin. Prick the base of the pastry all over with a fork. Bake blind for 15 minutes.
5 Beat the egg whites with the remaining sugar until stiff. Gently fold the egg whites into the lemon cream then pour this mixture into the pastry case. Bake at 180°C/350°F/gas 4 for 20–25 minutes, until the surface is lightly browned all over. Serve the tart warm or cold.

SALADE D'ORANGES

Orange salad

INGREDIENTS

6 navel oranges
30ml (2 tbsps) orange-flower water
2 tbsps icing sugar
2 tsps ground cinnamon

PREPARATION

1 Peel the oranges and remove any pith. Slice them across very finely and arrange on a plate in overlapping circles.
2 Sprinkle over the orange-flower water, icing sugar and half the cinnamon. Chill the salad for at least 2 hours.
3 Just before serving, sprinkle the remaining cinnamon over the oranges.

FLAN DE NARANJA
Baked orange custard

The first orange groves planted in Spain yielded bitter oranges, which came to be known after the town of Seville. This delicate orange custard owes its special flavour to the inclusion of juice from a Seville orange as well as that from the more familiar sweet oranges.

INGREDIENTS

150g (5oz) white sugar
5 eggs
juice of 3 sweet oranges and 1 Seville orange,
approximately 450ml (¾ pint)
2 tsps orange-flower water, optional
1 tsp grated orange zest

PREPARATION

1 Mix 90g (3oz) of sugar with 2 teaspoons of water in a saucepan. Warm over a medium heat until the sugar has caramelized and become a light golden colour. Do not let it burn.
2 Pour the caramelized sugar into the base of a 20cm (8in) oval flan dish or a 18cm (7in) round dish (you could also use 4 individual dishes).
3 To make the custard, whisk the eggs with the remaining sugar until light and creamy. Carefully stir in the orange juice, orange-flower water, if using, and zest.
4 Preheat the oven to 150°C/300°F/gas 2. Pour the custard into the flan dish, and then place this in a baking tray filled with sufficient warm water to come halfway up the side of the dish.
5 Bake the custard in the oven for 1 hour, until it is set and a skewer inserted into it comes out clean. Leave to cool completely before turning it out onto a serving dish. The custard should be topped with a layer of runny caramel.

RAHAT LOKUM
Turkish delight

This sweet, sticky treat was for centuries the delight of the women of the harems. Serve with cardamom coffee.

INGREDIENTS

500g (1lb) white sugar
juice of ½ lemon
30g (1oz) powdered gelatine
½ tsp vanilla essence
30ml (2 tbsps) rose-water
butter, to coat baking tray
60g (2oz) blanched pistachio nuts, chopped
60g (2oz) icing sugar
30g (1oz) cornflour

PREPARATION

1 Mix the white sugar and 300ml (10fl oz) of water in a saucepan. Add the lemon juice. Heat slowly to dissolve the sugar, then bring to the boil.
2 Continue to boil until the temperature reaches 125°C (250°F) on a sugar thermometer, or until a little dropped into cold water forms a hard ball. Take the syrup off the heat. Do not allow it to caramelize.
3 Place the pan in a bowl of iced water and leave to cool for 10 minutes.
4 Dissolve the gelatine in 125ml (4fl oz) of hot water. Stir the gelatine, vanilla essence and rose-water into the syrup.
5 Lightly butter a 15cm (6in) baking tray. Pour in half the syrup then sprinkle with nuts. Cover with the remaining syrup and leave to cool. When cool, place in the refrigerator for 24 hours.
6 Cut the set mixture into squares. Sift together the icing sugar and cornflour and roll the squares in it. Leave to dry on a tray for 24 hours. Store in an airtight container.

SEPHARDI TAMAR
Stuffed dates

Fresh dates are made even more luxurious in Israel, where they are stoned and stuffed with a nugget of almond-flavoured paste. This little sweetmeat is perfect with a cup of coffee.

INGREDIENTS

16 fresh dates
3 tbsps ground almonds
1 tbsp finely chopped pistachio nuts
1 tbsp caster sugar
30g (1oz) unsalted butter, softened

PREPARATION

1 With a sharp knife, make a slit down the centre of each date and carefully remove the stone.
2 Mix together the almonds, pistachio nuts, sugar and butter, adding a very little water so that you have a smooth paste.
3 Fashion the paste into nuggets the size of date stones and use these to stuff the dates. Chill thoroughly before serving.

VARIATION

• Pour a syrup of 125g (4oz) white sugar, 2 tbsps clear honey, 30ml (2 tbsps) lemon juice and 175ml (6fl oz) of water over the dates, then chill.

BAKLAVA

Pastry with nuts

The original baklava *was made up of 40 sheets of pastry, symbolizing the 40 days of Lent, and was traditionally eaten on Easter Day. Its popularity spread and baklava soon became a favourite with Turkish sultans, who relished the buttery pastry in its sweet sticky syrup.*

INGREDIENTS

200g (7oz) white sugar
4 tbsps clear honey
juice of ½ lemon
30ml (2 tbsps) rose-water
250g (8oz) unsalted butter
1 tsp cinnamon
375g (12oz) shelled, blanched walnuts, pistachios or almonds, roughly chopped
375g (12oz) packet filo pastry

PREPARATION

1 Put the sugar, honey, lemon juice and 450ml (¾ pint) of water in a pan and bring to the boil. Boil uncovered for 8–10 minutes, until the syrup is thick enough to coat the back of a spoon. Stir in the rose-water and leave to cool.

2 Melt the butter and skim off the scum that rises to the surface. Mix the cinnamon into the nuts. Preheat the oven to 180°C/350°F/gas 4.

3 Lay a sheet of pastry in a 30 x 18cm (12 x 7in) baking tray and brush with melted butter. Repeat with another 3 sheets, then sprinkle over a third of the nuts. Cover with 4 more sheets of pastry, brushing each time with butter, then add the second third of the nuts. Repeat the process with the remaining nuts and pastry, brushing the last piece liberally with butter.

4 With a sharp knife, make deep diagonal crosses across the top of the pastry to make lozenge shapes.

5 Bake the baklava for 30 minutes, then lower the oven temperature to 150°C/300°F/gas 2. Bake for a further 45 minutes, until the filo pastry is nicely browned.

6 Pour over the cool syrup, making sure plenty runs down between the cracks. Leave the baklava to cool before serving.

GRANITA DI COCOMERO

Watermelon granita

The Sicilians are credited with bringing the water-ice to Italy, having learnt the art of making it from their Arab invaders. The granita is closest to those original ices, being a frozen sherbet. This pale pink watermelon granita is a particular favourite in Sicily.

INGREDIENTS

1kg (2lb) slice of watermelon
250g (8oz) caster sugar
juice of ½ lemon
15ml (1 tbsp) orange-flower water
½ tsp ground cinnamon

PREPARATION

1 Remove the seeds and rind of the watermelon. Purée the flesh in a food processor.
2 Mix together the sugar and 150ml (¼ pint) of water and bring to the boil. Simmer for 5 minutes then take off the heat and stir in the lemon juice, orange-flower water and cinnamon. Leave to cool.
3 Combine the cooled syrup with the watermelon purée. Pour into a mould and place in the freezer.
4 Stir the mixture every 15 minutes for 2 hours, then every 30 minutes for a further hour, or until the granita has nearly frozen solid but still has a slightly slushy consistency. Serve, or if you wish to leave the granita in the freezer for longer, remove it an hour before serving so that it is not set solid.

MENU PLANNING

Mediterranean cooks do not tend to stick to rigid menus – what is chosen for a meal will in large part have been dictated by what was good in the market that day. This approach does require flexibility, but is invariably successful. The twelve menus here are intended to be inspirational, and include both ideas for regional themes and suggestions for specific social occasions.

PROVENCE

As you cook, the aromas of herbs and wine will evoke images of Provence in summer. This is a menu for the market shopper, using fresh produce cooked simply to allow flavour to shine through.

Soupe au Pistou (page 64)
Vegetable soup with pistou sauce *or*

Beignets de Fleurs de Courgette (page 84)
Courgette flower fritters with fresh tomato sauce

•

Loup de Mer Grillé au Fenouil (page 93)
Sea bass grilled with fennel *or*

Poulet Sauté aux Herbes de Provence (page 111)
Chicken sautéed with scrub herbs and garlic in white wine

Mesclun (page 77)
Salad of young leaves

•

Fraises de Bois au Vin Rouge (page 136)
Wild strawberries in red wine

SPAIN

This menu offers at the first and main course stage a choice of dishes from the Catalan and Andalusian coasts of Spain, two regions that guard their different culinary traditions jealously.

Escalivada (page 88)
Catalan roasted peppers, aubergines and onions *or*

Gazpacho Andaluz (page 36)
Andalusian gazpacho

•

Romesco de Peix (page 98)
Seafood stew with romesco pepper sauce *or*

Pato a la Sevillana (page 115)
Duck with olives, orange and sherry

Dulce de Membrillo (page 133) with Manchego cheese
Quince paste

•

Peras Estofados (page 134)
Poached pears

Poulet Sauté aux Herbes de Provence

Gazpacho Andaluz

ITALY

A traditional meal in Italy starts with antipasti, moves on to pasta, soup or a risotto and proceeds to the main course, often a simple grilled meat or fish dish. Fruit or ice-cream follows – then a siesta.

Bruschetta (page 120) with mixed salamis, pickled vegetables and olives
Garlic bread with antipasti

—•—

Gnocchi al Pesto (page 42)
Italian potato dumplings with pesto sauce **or**

Risotto di Carciofi (page 127)
Artichoke risotto

—•—

Zuppa di Pesce (page 34)
Italian fish soup **or**

La Pizzaiola (page 108)
Steak with tomato sauce

—•—

Pesche Ripiene (page 135)
Stuffed peaches

Zuppa di Pesce

NORTH AFRICA

North African food is ideal for large gatherings – a fragrant tagine and a couscous to which everyone helps themselves make for a convivial evening. Most of the menu can be made in advance.

Salata Jazar (page 74) with flat bread
Carrot salad

—•—

Tagine d'Agneau aux Abricots (page 118)
Tagine of lamb with apricots **or**

Djej Emshmel (page 46)
Tagine of chicken with lemons and olives

—•—

Couscous aux Sept Légumes (page 131)
Couscous with seven vegetables

—•—

Salade d'Oranges (page 136)
Orange salad

Djej Emshmel

GREECE AND TURKEY

These two countries may be separated only by the narrow Aegean Sea, but Greece has always looked west for its culinary inspiration while Turkey looks to the east. Their cuisines share much in common, but each remains distinctive.

Anginares me Koukia (page 76) with flat bread
Greek salad of artichokes with baby broad beans ***or***

Yoğurtlu Patlican (page 88)
Turkish fried aubergines with yogurt

·

Moussaka (page 114)
Baked aubergines layered with lamb ***or***

Iç Pilavi (page 130)
Pilav with chicken livers

·

Sika sto Fourno (page 134)
Baked figs ***or***

Baklava (page 138) and Rahat Lokum (page 137)
Pastry with nuts and Turkish delight

·

Turkish coffee

EASTERN MEDITERRANEAN

Meals in the east of the region usually start with a selection of little dishes eaten with bread. These *meze* are followed by meat or fish, often served with rice. Fresh fruit or marinated dried fruit are popular desserts.

Salata il Shamonder (page 74)
Beetroot salad

Baba Ghanoush (page 70)
Lebanese aubergine and sesame dip

Hummus bi Tahini (page 70)
Chick-pea and sesame dip

Tabbouleh (page 130) with lettuce and flat bread
Lebanese bulgur wheat and herb salad

·

Daoud Pasha (page 110)
Syrian spicy lamb meatballs with pine kernels in tomato sauce ***or***

Samak Meshwi bi Tahini (page 92) with rice
Grilled fish with sesame sauce

·

Khoshaf (page 136)
Dried fruit and nut salad

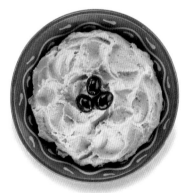

Baba Ghanoush

Baklava   *Hummus bi Tahini*

SUMMER LUNCH

On a hot summer's day, Mediterranean food comes into its own. You can prepare starters and desserts in advance and then leave some fish to bake in the oven or over the barbecue while you sit back and enjoy the sun.

Çaçik Soupa (page 60)
Cold soup of yogurt and cucumber *or*

Ratatouille (page 81) served cold
Vegetables stewed in olive oil

Rougets à la Niçoise (page 56)
Red mullet Niçois style *or*

Samak Charmoula (page 103)
Marinated and baked fish

Granita di Cocomero (page 139)
Watermelon granita

Rougets à la Niçoise

PICNIC

Combine a few easily transportable cooked dishes with some good country bread, a little cheese or salami and some luscious fresh fruit to refresh the palate and you have everything you need for a leisurely summer picnic.

Pan Bagnat (page 68)
Salade niçoise in a roll

Tortilla (page 85)
Spanish potato omelette

Pissaladière (page 48)
Provençal onion tart *or*

Spanakopita (page 89)
Spinach pie

Selection of goat's cheeses and salamis, with marinated olives and country bread

---

Fresh figs and grapes

Pan Bagnat

TECHNIQUES

Mediterranean food rarely requires complicated cooking techniques. Much of the cook's work is in the preparation of ingredients, perhaps trimming artichokes, preparing squid or spatchcocking chickens for the barbecue. This section demonstrates how quick and simple these tasks can be. An illustrated catalogue of equipment also features some of the traditional utensils found in Mediterranean kitchens and offers advice on choosing some of the more basic or indispensable items.

COOKING EQUIPMENT

A typical Mediterranean kitchen does not contain a great deal of specialist cooking equipment, but some basic items do make life appreciably easier, and may even help to improve the flavour of the food you are preparing. A few slightly more unusual pieces of equipment are also useful for specific dishes.

OTHER USEFUL EQUIPMENT
chopping board, marble or wooden; grinders for pepper and sea salt; coffee grinder, for coffee beans and whole spices; heat diffuser, to place on stove when using earthenware pans; wooden and slotted spoons; colander and sieves

Flat-blade skewers

SKEWERS
Flat-blade and round metal skewers are excellent for grilling and barbecuing meat or fish — the metal conducts the heat, ensuring that the food is cooked through. Wooden skewers can be used for small kebabs and for spatchcocking (see page 155).

POTS AND PANS
As a general rule, thick-based kitchenware suits the country-style cooking of much Mediterranean food. Unglazed earthenware pots give food a distinctive flavour — keep a round earthenware pot with handles to use over direct heat and several smaller round or oval dishes for baking. Enamelled casseroles are also useful. A large heavy cast-iron frying pan with a long handle is extremely versatile.

KNIVES
Use a small short-blade knife for vegetables and a larger knife with a long thick blade for meat, a small blunt knife for scaling fish and a mezza luna, a crescent-shaped, double-handled rocking knife for chopping herbs.

Mezza luna

Heavy cast-iron frying pan

Paellera

PAELLERA
The paellera is a shallow two-handled pan, traditionally made of iron. It is distinguished by its size — usually paellas are made in large quantities. Like all cast-iron utensils, it should be kept oiled when not in use.

COUSCOUSIER
This steamer allows you to cook the grains of couscous over the spicy stew with which they will be served.

EARTHENWARE CASSEROLE
An earthenware pot with a lid is excellent for oven cooking as it retains heat, flavour and moisture.

TAGINE
Used for the Moroccan stews to which it has lent its name, the tagine is an earthenware dish with a conical lid and a large round base.

PESTLE AND MORTAR
A large marble pestle and mortar is invaluable for pastes. Wooden and stone mortars can also be used. Choose a small mortar with a ridged base for crushing spices.

TIAN
The tian is a shallow oval earthenware dish, used for the various Provençal gratins to which it has lent its name (see page 103).

Grill pan's ridges score the food

GRILL PAN
A portable cast-iron grill pan allows you to cook Spanish-style on the hot plate.

PREPARING VEGETABLES

Certain vegetables need extra attention. Delicate salad leaves, for example, should be washed, then dried by shaking them in a tea towel, mushrooms should be wiped with a damp cloth – never immerse them in water.

SKINNING TOMATOES

Plunge the tomatoes in boiling water for 45 seconds, then drain. Pierce the skin at the top with a knife. Score to the bottom then peel off the skin. To deseed tomatoes, cut them in half lengthways and scoop out the seeds.

PEELING RED PEPPERS

Preheat the grill to maximum. Grill the pepper, turning it frequently, until the skin is thoroughly blackened, about 20 minutes. Remove and cover with a clean tea towel for 10 minutes, then peel off the blistered skin with your fingers.

SALTING AND BLOTTING

Certain vegetables, such as aubergines and courgettes, have bitter juices. This process draws them out. Slice the vegetables as instructed in the recipe. Place in a colander and sprinkle with coarse salt, about 2 tsps per aubergine, 1 tsp per courgette. Cover with a plate and place a heavy weight on top. Leave to drain for 30–45 minutes. Rinse well and pat dry with kitchen paper.

MAKING SAUCES

Cold sauces, such as pesto, are best made in a pestle and mortar. Pound the first elements, often garlic and sea salt, until they break down. Add the remaining ingredients and crush to make a paste.

PREPARING ARTICHOKES

1 Peel back the tough outer leaves of the artichoke so that they snap off. (This is the only necessary preparation technique for baby artichokes.)

2 Using a sharp knife, slice horizontally through the leaves 2.5cm (1in) from the base of the artichoke.

3 Cut the stalk off at the base. Scrape out the small central leaves and hairy "choke" and discard. Rinse, then place in acidulated water (see page 156).

DOUGH AND PASTRY

Variations of bread dough are used in many regional specialities, from Pissaladière (see page 48) to pizzas. The preparation techniques are broadly similar.

Pastry, too, requires a few basic skills that are applicable to a wide range of dishes. Filo pastry is an art form in itself to make; the ready-made frozen product is excellent.

KNEADING AND KNOCKING BACK DOUGH

1 Prepare the dough according to the recipe. Flour your hands and begin to work the dough on a floured surface, pressing the dough with your knuckles and turning it over and over.

2 When the dough loses its stickiness and reaches a smooth, pliable consistency, place it in an oiled bowl, cover with a clean tea towel, and leave in a warm place to rise.

3 When the dough has doubled in size (approximately 1 hour), lightly press it back, or "knock back", with your knuckles to expel the air. Some recipes will require you to work it again.

MAKING FILO PASTRY TRIANGLES

1 Place a strip of pastry on a dry surface. Brush with melted or clarified butter. Place some filling on the bottom right-hand corner, about 2cm (¾in) from the edge. Pick up the corner.

2 Fold the bottom right-hand corner over the filling to make a triangle. Carefully pick up the corner of the triangle in your thumb and forefinger, keeping the filling intact.

3 Continue folding the triangle across and up the strip, being careful not to lose any filling, until you reach the end of the strip.

Crisp filo pastry parcels

4 Brush the triangle with melted or clarified butter, then bake.

FISH AND SHELLFISH

Make a friend of your fishmonger and you will receive expert advice on what is best from the catch of the day and assistance in its preparation. If you do have to gut and clean fish yourself, make sure you wash them out thoroughly.

When buying shellfish, choose raw whole prawns and cook and peel them yourself. Mediterranean cooks usually buy crabs and lobsters alive and cook them at home to ensure freshness – if you buy them ready-cooked, ask when they were prepared.

CLEANING FISH

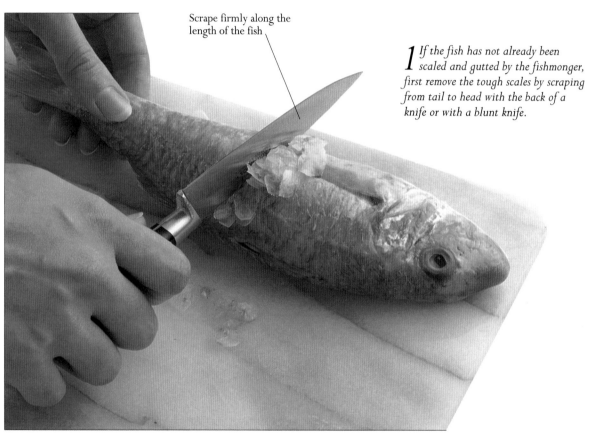

Scrape firmly along the length of the fish

1 If the fish has not already been scaled and gutted by the fishmonger, first remove the tough scales by scraping from tail to head with the back of a knife or with a blunt knife.

2 Using a small sharp knife, make a slit up along the length of the belly to the gills. Cut off the gills.

3 Grasp the innards between your thumb and forefinger and pull them out of the cavity.

4 Holding the fish open, rinse the belly cavity under cold running water to remove traces of blood.

PREPARING SQUID

1 Clutch the base of the head and pull out the attached innards from the body sac. Discard the head and innards and rinse the body inside and out.

2 Cut off the tentacles just below the eyes, taking care to remove the hard inedible "beak", and set aside.

3 Peel off the mottled outer skin, together with the "wings", to reveal the milky white flesh.

4 Pull out the transparent plastic-like "bone" that runs vertically along the body sac. Wash well again. Cut up the tentacles and white flesh as described in the recipe.

CLEANING MUSSELS AND CLAMS

1 Place mussels and clams in salted water to allow them to disgorge grit. Discard any that fail to open or are broken.

2 Scrub the shellfish with a small stiff brush to remove any barnacles or dirt attached to the outer shell.

3 For mussels, pull out the small strands that protrude from one side of the shell. This is known as "debearding".

CLEANING SCALLOPS

1 Scallops are tricky to open and prepare. If you do buy uncleaned scallops, prise the shell halves apart with a small blunt knife. Be careful not to damage the flesh.

2 With a sharp knife, cut the white muscle away from the shell, then cut off the inedible membranes. Keep the edible coral intact. Rinse all traces of grit away under cold running water.

The scallop is now ready to be cooked on the shell under a grill, or cooked separately and then returned to its shell.

MEAT

The way that animals are reared, fed, slaughtered, hung and finally prepared for the table affects the taste of the meat — look for a good butcher to help you find the best products. Corn-fed chickens, for example, have the best flavour, and game that has been hung is far more tender. If you are barbecuing meat, leave on a little fat as it provides flavour and keeps in moisture during cooking. When roasting a joint of meat, allow it to rest for 10–15 minutes before carving and serving it.

JOINTING CHICKEN

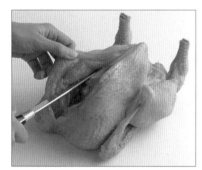

1 Make an incision down the breast-bone towards the tail end. Cut down the side of the breastbone to loosen the flesh. Remove the wishbone.

2 Cut down until you reach the wing joint, then slice through it. Put the point of your knife in the wing socket and push away the breast.

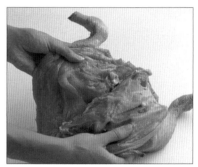

3 Begin to separate the whole side from the frame of the carcass by cutting downwards through the skin and flesh then pulling away the side.

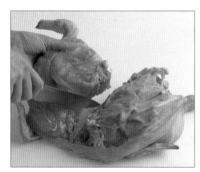

4 Cut down through the leg joint, and break it away from the main carcass, then cut away the whole side.

5 Cut around the thigh and leg joint, separating it from the breast and wing. Remove the wing tips and discard.

6 Cut away the wing, leaving a little breast attached. Make a cut between the thigh and drumstick, then divide.

Chicken jointed into 8 pieces

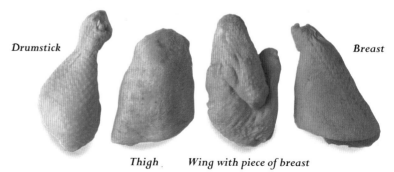

Drumstick   **Breast**

Thigh   **Wing with piece of breast**

7 Repeat with the other side. You now have 8 joints of chicken. For 16 pieces, chop both the legs and thighs in half, chop both breast pieces in half again, and add the parson's nose from the carcass and the wishbone.

SPATCHCOCKING SMALL BIRDS

1 Place the bird on a cutting board breast-side down. With a sharp knife, split the bird by cutting all the way along the backbone.

2 Turn the bird the other way up and flatten it out by pressing down on the breastbone with the heel of your hand in order to crack it.

3 Secure the bird flat by pushing a skewer through it from the wing tip on one side to the leg on the other. Repeat.

SKEWERING MINCED MEAT KEBABS

1 Dampen your hands with water before handling the minced meat. Take a piece the size of an egg and mould it around the centre of the skewer – flat blades are best (see page 148).

2 Moisten your hands again and then stretch out the mixture along the length of the skewer, lightly pressing it into shape, until you have a sausage about 10cm (4in) long.

The kebabs are now ready to be cooked under the grill or on the barbecue. Cover with clingfilm until needed.

STOCK

A stock is an infusion of flavours into a liquid, usually water. Fish, meat and vegetable stocks are very basic descriptions: there is a great difference between a shellfish and a fish stock or a beef and a chicken stock. Stocks can be light or strong, depending on how heavily they have been reduced. It is worth making stock whenever you have excess vegetables, a few fish heads or some bones. Stock freezes well and bought stock cubes are no replacement.

TO MAKE A STOCK

Place the fish or shellfish trimmings, vegetables or meat bones in a pan and cover with water. Add flavourings such as herbs, spices, 1 or 2 glasses of wine, and onion, according to the main ingredient. Bring to the boil, then reduce to a slow simmer. Leave to cook uncovered. The longer the stock cooks, the more intense its flavour will be. If you wish to strengthen the flavour, boil hard to reduce it at the end of the simmering period. Always salt stock at the end of reducing – the saltiness is intensified as the stock reduces – and skim off any fat or impurities.

Fish stock should never be cooked for more than 40 minutes or it will make glue.

Meat stock will be more flavourful if the bones are first roasted. Cook for at least 2 hours.

Vegetable stock is improved if the vegetables are first fried in a little oil. Cook for at least 1 hour.

GLOSSARY

ACIDULATED WATER

Water can be made acid by the addition of lemon juice or vinegar and used to cover prepared vegetables, for example globe artichokes, before cooking, to prevent discoloration.

AL DENTE

This phrase meaning "to the tooth" is used to describe the moment when pasta is ready, i.e. when it is tender but still offers some resistance. The exact moment when pasta becomes *al dente* is a matter of personal taste, and varies according to the type and freshness of the pasta – taste to check.

BLANCHING

Certain ingredients can be "blanched" before use by being scalded or parboiled in boiling water. This process may be used to whiten and/or remove skin, as with almonds, or to remove excess bitterness or saltiness, as with black olives.

BOUQUET GARNI

A bouquet garni is a bunch of herbs used to flavour a slow-cooking dish. Ready prepared bouquet garnis filled with dried herbs are worse than useless – tie fresh or dried herbs together at the stalk or do not include a bouquet garni at all.

CLARIFIED BUTTER

Butter that is to be used for brushing filo pastry should first be melted, producing a scum that can be skimmed off. This process removes impurities, producing clear or "clarified" butter.

DOUBLE BOILER

A double boiler, usually consisting of a heat-proof bowl placed over a pan of simmering water, is used when it is essential that ingredients do not come into direct contact with the heat source, for example when making an egg-based sauce, where exposure to direct heat might cause curdling or separation.

DRY FRYING

Spices are best kept whole and roasted, "dry fried", in the frying pan as needed. Place a dry frying pan over a medium heat until it is hot. Add the whole spices and fry, stirring constantly, for 1 minute, until lightly browned and fragrant. Ensure that the spices do not burn, and allow to cool before grinding.

EMULSIFICATION

An emulsification is an amalgamation by whisking of two liquids of different gravities, as with oil and vinegar or egg yolks and oil. To facilitate this process, the liquids should be at room temperature.

LARDONS

Used to flavour casseroles and soups, lardons are small strips of pork fat, pancetta or bacon.

SALTING AND BLOTTING

Some vegetables, like the aubergine and courgette, contain bitter juices that need to be extracted before cooking. They should be salted and weighted down to draw out these juices, according to the instructions on page 150.

SOFREGIT

A *sofregit* is the foundation of many Catalan dishes, and the phrase "first make a sofregit" is a common instruction in Catalan cooking. At its simplest, it consists of onions, tomatoes, perhaps with herbs and garlic, stewed in olive oil until very soft. The other ingredients in the dish are then added to this fundamental flavouring combination. The Castilian *sofrito* and the Italian *soffritto* are similar.

NOTES

QUANTITIES

Recipes are designed to make 4 generous servings, unless otherwise stated.

OVEN TEMPERATURES

The temperatures given in centigrade are for conventional rather than fan ovens, which cook food more quickly.

MEASUREMENTS

Quantities are given in both imperial and metric. Be careful not to mix the versions within one recipe.

TASTING

Always taste the dish regularly during preparation, not just at the very end of cooking, and adjust seasoning and herbs to your preference.

INDEX

ACKNOWLEDGMENTS

Author's acknowledgments
With grateful thanks to my parents for introducing me to the food and way of life of the Mediterranean at an early age; to my husband Jonathan for sharing with me a passion for the region and its cooking; and above all to the many people who over the years have taken me into their kitchens and generously given me their family recipes. And of course special thanks to Clive Streeter, Janice Murfitt and Dave King, and all the team at Dorling Kindersley, especially Lorna and Jo, for their hard work in making the book look so splendid.

Dorling Kindersley would like to thank Clive Streeter for his generous help and enthusiasm and Janice Murfitt, our home economist, for her hard work. Special thanks also to home economists Deborah Greatrex, Sunil Vijayakar, Kerenza Harries and Kathy Man; Alison Stace for hand modelling; Hilary Guy and Ayisha de Lanerolle for styling assistance; Artemi Kyriacou for photographic assistance; Sarah Ereira for the index; Amanda Ursell for nutritional advice; Sasha Kennedy and Emy Mamby for design assistance and Nick Turpin for editorial assistance.
With thanks to the following companies and individuals for their assistance: The National Fruit Collection, Brogdale; Cool Chile Company; Steve Hatt, Lina Stores, Randall & Aubin and Hyams and Cockerton, London. Many thanks to the following for kindly loaning equipment and props: Elizabeth David Cookshop, The Kasbah and Pages Catering Equipment, London; Mr. H. Leatherland.
Picture credits: Photography by Clive Streeter except Dave King: pages 2-3, 12-29, 55, 135, 140bl.